Where's the Faucet?

"A Journey from Pressure to Purpose -

and the Leadership Lessons That Pour from It"

By Christopher M. Card Jr

Copyright © 2025 by The Overflow Group

All rights reserved.

No portion of this book may be reproduced, stored in a retrieval system, or transmitted in any form or by any means—electronic, mechanical, photocopying, recording, scanning, or otherwise—without prior written permission from the publisher, except for brief quotations used in reviews, articles, or scholarly works.

For permission requests, contact:

The Overflow Group

Las Vegas, Nevada

ISBN: 979-8993367408

Printed in the United States of America

Cover Design: Christopher M Card Jr

Book Design: The Overflow Group

This is a work of creative nonfiction. Some names and identifying details have been changed to protect the privacy of individuals. Events have been portrayed as truthfully as memory and documentation allow.

All rights reserved worldwide.

Dedication & Acknowledgments

Thank You

To my friends, family, coaches, colleagues, and even strangers—your presence in my life, whether brief or long-standing, intentional or accidental, helped shape me. Some of you gave advice. Others gave time. Some offered hard truths. And a few gave grace when I hadn't yet earned it.

There are too many to name, but two deserve to be spoken aloud here:

Tamiko Judge — for your relentless love and unshakable strength.

Christopher Card Sr. — for showing me that a quiet man can make a loud impact.

You both are woven into every chapter of my becoming.

To My Flower and My Children — When life ever seems to run dry, all I have to do is look at you, and I find my flow again. You will forever be my heart — the living evidence of everything I ever prayed for.

Because of you, I choose to be more.

Because of you, I found the faucet.

Above all else, Thank You, **God** — because of You, my cup truly runneth over.

-Christopher M Card Jr

Table of Contents

The Framework: Before you Begin

PART I – THE LEAKS: WHERE IT ALL STARTED

A story of Pressure, Presence, and the Pain that watered the roots of a Leader

1. Born Without the Faucet
2. Pressure Points
3. The Name I Inherited
4. Worlds Collide
5. Us Against the World.
6. The Flood or the Drought
7. When the Ball Dropped
8. From Cracks to Collapse

Reflection Exercise: Find the Faucet Within

Table of Contents

PART II – THE BLUEPRINT: HOW I STARTED BUILDING

A journey from survival to structure — where leadership became less about personality and more about purpose

   9. The Interview That Changed Everything
   10. My First Faucet
   11. Forged in Fire
   12. Success Without Inclusion is Still Failure
   13. The Pilot
   14. When the Leaks Return
   15. A Seat at the Table

Reflective Questions & Mid-Chapter Pause & Pour Moments

Table of Contents

PART III – THE POUR

Leadership that Multiplies — Pouring into People, Process, and Purpose

16. When the Faucet Pours

17. Permission to Pour

18. From Shadow to Source

19. Altitude

20. When the World Tilted

21. Rebuilding From the Ground Up

22. When the Veils Lift

23. From Contractor to Architect

24. Leading Through Discomfort

25. Where the Faucet Leads

26. The Reflection in the Mirror

Table of Contents

PART IV – THE PRACTICE: THE BLUEPRINT IN MOTION

From story to system — the frameworks that keep the faucet flowing

- 27. From Story to System
- 28. The Leaks (LEAK Framework)
- 29. Where Is the Faucet? (FAUCET Framework)
- 30. Resistance Isn't Rebellion (BRIDGE Model)
- 31. Self-Calibrating the Container (C.L.E.A.R. Alignment)
- 32. The Living System
- 33. The Unfinished Climb
- 34. Legacy Impact
- 35. The Final Pour

Closing Remarks

Note of Thanks

About the Author

Stay Connected

Table of Contents

Appendix: Leadership Worksheets & Tools

- LEAK Framework Worksheet
- FAUCET Action Planner
- C.L.E.A.R. Self-Check
- BRIDGE Coaching Template
- Legacy & Pour Plan Tracker
- Operational & Leadership Glossary

The Framework: Before You Begin

This isn't a book you read—it's one you walk through. Every chapter in *Where's the Faucet?* carries two things: story and system. You'll move through childhood pressure, corporate boardrooms, and moments of spiritual reflection. But what ties it all together is one truth: **leadership and life are never separate.**

The leaks you've patched in your personal life often show up in your professional one. The courage it takes to lead others is the same courage it takes to face yourself. The systems that build businesses can also rebuild people.

This book is layered. It moves through *The Leaks, The Blueprint, The Pour,* and *The Practice*—each part revealing a new stage of growth: from surviving to building, from building to multiplying, from multiplying to sustaining.

This book will ask things of you. You'll find **Pause & Pour** reflections designed to stop you mid-read, challenge your assumptions, and stir something deeper than motivation.

The frameworks—**LEAK, FAUCET, CLEAR, BRIDGE**—aren't corporate models. They're human blueprints. They help you diagnose, realign, and pour with purpose—in your work, your relationships, your parenting, and your faith. Because the question *Where Is the Faucet?* was never about water. It's about the source. About alignment. About finding the place within you that keeps pouring even when life runs dry.

So take a breath- This isn't the beginning of a book—*it's the beginning of your becoming.*

Part I – *THE LEAKS:*

WHERE IT ALL STARTED

A story of pressure, presence, and the pain that watered the roots of a leader

Chapter 1: Born Without the Faucet

Before I had words, I had awareness.

Not the kind of awareness a child is supposed to carry—the kind that watches how long the fridge stays empty or how quiet a room goes when the rent's overdue. I carried a knowing. I don't remember the moment it arrived. It was just always there, like background noise I learned to translate before I could even write my name.

In first grade, I went to live with my aunt. I saw my parents in fragments—visits, check-ins, "be good for your TT." I was old enough to understand that I was safe, but young enough to notice I wasn't home. The kids at school seemed to live in pictures I didn't have. They brought in family photos—Christmas cards with mom and dad holding them between matching pajamas or posed by a tree. I didn't have a single picture of me with both of my parents. Not one. The only image I ever saw of us together was one my grandmother had—a photo of me as a newborn, cradled between two people who hadn't yet figured out how to hold each other.

My parents were both beautiful contradictions. My mom—Black, brilliant, blunt—loved hard because she had no other choice. She was raised by her grandmother, fought through lupus, heartbreak, abandonment, and learned to mother us in the absence of knowing how to mother herself. She taught me early: **pressure is a privilege**. Her love wasn't coddling—it was calling. Calling me to rise, to take responsibility, to help carry the weight she never asked for but refused to drop.

My dad was the quiet strength to her fire. White, blue-collar, a man of tools and talent. He rarely told me his story, but others did—stories of poverty, of hustle, of redemption. He was respected everywhere we went. Never boastful, but never invisible either. His silence wasn't distance; it was dignity. When I was with him, it felt like a break in the noise. We'd sit in silence and watch TV. It wasn't much—but it was peace. And for a man who worked thirteen-hour days, six days a week, I eventually understood what that silence cost—and what it meant for him to share it with me.

The leaks were everywhere in my early life—unstable housing, fractured family, love that had to work overtime to feel like enough. **But even then, the faucet hadn't been found.** I just knew I was thirsty. I just didn't know what for.

Chapter 2: Pressure Points

The earliest leadership lesson I ever got didn't come from a book—it came from my mom handing me someone else's punishment.

When my younger siblings got in trouble, I'd get in trouble too. I didn't hit them. I didn't break the rule. But she'd look at me, with that sharp wisdom in her eyes, and say: "If you knew better, you should've stopped them."

At the time, it pissed me off. I was a kid, just like them. But she wasn't raising just a kid—she was raising a protector, a leader, a guardian. Someone who didn't just watch over people, but made things better just by being there. That expectation shaped me. So did the reward that sometimes followed.

Once a year, we had "Big Brother's Day." A day just for me. A thank-you for being the oldest. For stepping up. One year in particular still lives in my soul. We went to the Boulevard Mall. She bought me my first pair of Jordans, a hot dog on a stick, and we went to the movies—just the two of us. We sat and talked for hours. She told me she saw me, valued me, and needed me. That I made life better for my siblings and for her. That day, I didn't feel the weight of leadership. I felt the worth.

But there were also days that felt like the world could flip with one bad mood. I remember one night—we were staying at my mom's best friend's house. My mom was cleaning hard before she got home. I was eating a PB&J in the kitchen when the door slammed. Voices raised. Tension climbed. Within moments, my mom burst into the room, grabbed our things, and said we had to leave. Just like that, we were in the car with nowhere to go. That's when I learned that even love isn't always enough. People can change, and so can your address.

That night taught me something vital: **emotions dictate environments**. That would shape how I led people decades later. I learned early—mood management could be the difference between peace and panic, home and homelessness.

Chapter 3: The Name I Inherited

There was a day I found out who I was—and it wasn't when I was born.

I was six. My mom had been dressing me and my younger brother the same—matching fits like we were twins. I hated it. I told her I wanted to be my own person. She told my dad.

That weekend, when he picked me up, our first stop wasn't home—it was a shop. He bought me a custom beanie and shirt stitched with the words "Lil Chris." I asked why it said that. He said, "Because you're my son. You're a Jr."

I'd always heard people call him "Mike," and it never clicked. But in that moment, standing in a shop with my name stitched in thread, I felt identity settle into my skin. I didn't just come from him. I carried him. His name, his path, his story.

That pride never left me. Not because I wanted to be him, but because I realized I came from something. And maybe I could take the story further.

Years later, just before things fell apart between us, we were driving home from football practice. Out of nowhere, he asked, "Do you think I'm successful?"

I answered quickly. "Yeah. You're the first in your family to graduate, you own a home, people respect you…"

He held out his hands and said, "Feel these."

They were callused. Scarred. Worn.

He said, "I get paid for what I do with my hands. But I'll know I succeeded when you get paid for what you do with your mind."

That was the moment something inside me shifted. I saw legacy not as inheritance, but as evolution.

He was building with bricks.

I would build with blueprints.

Chapter 4: Worlds Collide

My life split early between two homes—and two Americas.

At Mom's, we lived on faith, finesse, and food stamps. In Dad's world, we had stability, structure, and spaghetti dinners around a clean table. Same kid, different planets.

Switching between them wasn't just packing a bag—it was becoming a different version of myself. At my mom's, I was the man of the house. I watched my siblings while she worked graveyard shifts, learned to stretch a box of cereal across four days, and negotiated bedtime like a lawyer. At my dad's, I was the kid—quiet, clean, out the way. His wife set house rules I didn't know I was breaking just by existing: no extra cleaning, no babysitting, no backtalk. But I always felt like I was one toe out of bounds. And the moment I misstepped? It was made known.

Christmas became the measuring stick. At Dad's, gifts flooded the living room—video games, sneakers, brand-new bikes. At Mom's, some years there was just a card, maybe socks, maybe nothing. I knew it wasn't her fault. I knew she gave what she could. Still, I felt it. That ache of comparison.

One year, I invented something called "Santa's Brother." A made-up tradition just for us, where gifts came not on December 25th but when I returned. I'd bring back a few of the presents I got at Dad's and rewrap them for my siblings. It wasn't charity—it was ritual. Something sacred I could give. A way to make Christmas feel like it came after all. My Mom leaned into it, too. But deep down, I think it gave her peace to watch her kids unwrap joy—even if it was borrowed.

Living between those two worlds taught me how to read a room, shift tones, blend in. It taught me that **leadership doesn't start with authority—it starts with adaptation**. You don't control the faucet unless you know how to move through droughts and storms.

Chapter 5: Us Against the World

My siblings weren't just family, they were my first team.

And I was the captain, whether I asked for it or not.

One day around 9 or 10, I got tired of daycare. Tired of the bland dinners, the early bedtimes, and being under someone else's schedule. I asked my mom, "How much are you paying for this?" She gave me the number. I did the math. "You could save that if you just let me watch us."

That was the pitch. I made it convincing, mature, and bulletproof. And she agreed.

For a few years, I took on the role: brother, babysitter, co-parent. I made sure they were fed, the lights were off when mom mandated, and that the house stayed intact. We watched movies, played games, and learned to laugh through the struggle. But eventually, life added pressure. My mom lost her mom. She got breast cancer on top of the lupus. Her health took a dramatic slip.

Stress became the soundtrack. And that's when the cracks deepened.

People talk about maturity like it's a medal. But mine was a shield. I used responsibility as a hiding place, from chaos, from grief, from the fear of being powerless. But shields get heavy. And eventually, I couldn't carry it all.

Still, those years taught me something I'd never trade: **leadership begins in the quiet sacrifices no one sees**. It's making things better because you can, not because you have to. It's love in motion

Chapter 6: The Flood or the Drought

Some floods destroy. Some droughts define. But both will teach you who you are when the water is gone.

At 11 years old, I learned that one small decision could shift the course of everything—and that doing the right thing, with the wrong timing, could still cost you everything.

It was Halloween night. My mom had arranged for my older cousin to take me and my siblings trick-or-treating. He was late. I was impatient. I wanted my little brother and sister to feel normal for once—to dress up, to laugh, to get candy like the rest of the kids. So I stepped up. Got my siblings ready. Took them out myself.

The next morning, November 1st, the consequences came knocking. A neighbor saw the kids home alone while my mom was still at work. The police showed up. By the time I got home, it was already in motion. They didn't ask questions. They didn't care about the why.

I remember sitting in the intake office, cold fluorescent lights buzzing above me, while my siblings were separated into the "young minors" area. A cop mocked me—called me Mr. Mom—because I knew all my siblings' allergies and birthdays. Like that was weird. Like that kind of care was too soft to be taken seriously.

I wasn't proud. I was ashamed. And in that moment, I felt the first deep wave of survivor's guilt. I wasn't taken to foster care. My dad came and got me. But my siblings? They stayed. In tents. With strangers. I sat in that lobby alone, trying to make sense of how doing the right thing—protecting, leading, stepping up—could leave me feeling so wrong.

That's when I started to believe life wasn't happening for me. It was happening to me.

And I carried that weight for years.

Chapter 7: When the Ball Dropped

Sports were my first love—and my first escape.

When I moved in with my dad around age 12, my world changed. For the first time, I had consistency. A bed I didn't have to share. A fridge I didn't have to negotiate. A sense of calm, even if it came with its own challenges. I was still the same kid who had been taking care of his siblings, still carrying that guilt from Halloween night, but I finally had space to be something else. Something more.

That's when I found sports.

Football, especially, became more than a game to me. It was structure. Brotherhood. A space where effort translated into outcome. The weight I had carried for so long got rechanneled into discipline. Into reps. Into wins.

I wasn't the fastest. I wasn't the strongest. But I saw the game differently. I had vision. The kind of vision that lets you see the field and everyone on it—and lead them, not just by calling plays, but by setting tone. By example.

I became a captain. Not just on paper, but in presence. People listened. Leaders trusted me. Teammates followed me.

Off the field, I found my voice too. I became class president. The kid who once felt invisible now had a mic. A platform. I started learning how to navigate different worlds—could sit with the athletes, speak with the teachers, lead a classroom or a huddle.

For a moment, everything was aligning.

Sports gave me an identity. And more importantly, it gave me belonging.

But just as quickly as that world came together, it all started to unravel.

Home life got shaky again. The tension that had quieted began to rise. At 16, I got kicked out. Football season was done—no warning, no senior send-off, no closure. Just me, a backpack, and a list of places I hoped would let me crash.

I bounced between couches. Friends. Cousins. One of those cousins was already waist-deep in the hustle. I won't glamorize it, but I can't lie—it was magnetic. That life promised fast money, power, control. All the things I thought I had lost when football slipped through my hands.

I went from Friday night lights to dim motel hallways on Boulder Highway.

From game film and playbooks to survival and silence.

That place was its own kind of classroom. The people I met there? Some had everything and lost it. Others had nothing and still offered you their last dollar. I saw addicts who still had dreams. Immigrants who were building empires one shift at a time. Moms raising three kids alone. Hustlers who read you like a book.

It's where I learned to code-switch without flinching. Where I sharpened my instinct for reading rooms, reading people, and moving accordingly. That skill would become one of my greatest assets later in life—but back then, it was just armor.

And underneath all that? I was grieving. Not just the loss of football—but the version of myself I thought I was building.

There's no locker room speech for when real life hits.

No halftime adjustment when your team is gone and the lights are off.

At 16, I stood at a crosswalk one night and watched a limo roll by—my old teammates inside, headed to prom. They were dressed sharp, laughing, headed to a night I thought I'd earned. Behind that limo was my reality:

A job on the Strip. A shift starting in two hours. A backpack full of clothes I'd rotate at bus stops.

That moment hit like a freight train. It wasn't just that I missed prom. It was that I was no longer part of that story. My chapter had ended—and no one warned me the page was about to turn.

I didn't have the language for it then. But I do now:

That's the moment when the ball dropped.

I realized everything I had—every gift, opportunity, moment of favor—could be gone in an instant.

And everything I thought I lost was actually teaching me how to lead.

Those setbacks? They weren't punishments. They were principles.

- That Halloween night? Leadership under pressure.
- Getting mocked by a cop? Learning that care is powerful, even when it goes unrecognized.

- Being spared while others weren't? That guilt became my fire.
- Losing the life I loved? That's when purpose started whispering.

These weren't just events. They were blueprints.

And at the time, I didn't even know I was building.

What I did know was this:

I didn't have a faucet.

I was praying for rain.

Chapter 8: From Cracks to Collapse

After the ball dropped, life didn't slow down. It just got quieter.

The noise of the field was gone. So was the team. What replaced it was a silence that settled in deep—and never really left. I wasn't on Boulder Highway anymore, but the survival mindset came with me. It followed me to every couch, every shift, every missed opportunity I was too tired or too jaded to chase.

By now, I had mastered the surface-level game: hustle, charm, results. I could make it look easy. But under the surface, I was leaking. My cup had cracks—and the pressure I'd carried for years was starting to burst through them.

Emotionally, my outlet was silence. I cried in private. Wiped my face. Came back out smiling. Not because I was faking, but because there was no other choice. When you're the one everyone leans on, there's no space to fall apart. I made solitude my sanctuary. My own silent altar.

And even though I wasn't raised in church, God was everywhere.

My grandmother was an evangelist. My mom used to preach in the living room with just me as her congregation. I didn't know scripture, but I knew presence. I knew reverence. I knew the stillness that wrapped around you when you had no words left.

One of the most perspective-shifting moments during that time didn't come from a sermon or a breakdown—it came from a kid.

He couldn't have been older than ten. Lived a few doors down from where I was staying at the time. His mother had left him when he was five, and he'd been taking care of his disabled father ever since. No adults. No stability. Just him. I'd watch him carry groceries, help his dad bathe, cut his food, all while trying to flip the little they had—usually his dad's disability check—just to keep the lights on.

At an age where most kids are worried about homework or recess, he was worried about rent. At ten.

That kid showed me something I hadn't really grasped yet:

It wasn't just my life that was hard.

It wasn't just my story that was heavy.

There were people all around me carrying weights I couldn't even imagine—and doing it with grit, love, and zero applause.

It broke something in me. But it also built something. It gave me range. It humbled my pain. It reminded me not to let struggle make me self-centered.

Because while I was leaking from pressure, he was drowning in it.

And still—he showed up. That image of him, small in body but massive in spirit, still lives in me.

Watching that young boy hold down a broken household? That was when I stopped seeing pain as personal—and started seeing it as **a shared language**. This would be massive in my career and creating a people first culture.

I came to believe something simple but sacred:

There are no neutral moments.

They're either breaking you, building you—or both at once.

Eventually, the floods taught me to let go.

And the droughts?

They taught me to dig.

To dig for peace when success didn't show up.

To dig for healing when nobody apologized.

To dig for vision when all I had was memory.

That's how I started to find something deeper than survival.

That's how I found the faucet.

Pause & Pour: Part I Reflection Exercise

Before you turn the page, sit with these questions.

Write them out. Pray on them. Revisit them. Let them work on you.

1. **What moment in your life once felt like punishment, but you now realize was preparation?**

   - *What did it strip from you?*
   - *What did it plant in you?*

2. **Where have you led out of love—but paid a price for it?**

   - *Did it change the way you lead now?*
   - *Was the cost worth it?*

3. **Who poured into you when your cup was cracked?**

   - *Have you thanked them?*
   - *Can you do for someone else what they once did for you?*

4. **When did survival become your identity?**

   - *How is that helping—or hurting—you now?*
   - *What does thriving look like for the version of you today?*

**"The question isn't whether the glass is half full or half empty.
It's: Where's the faucet?"**

You've seen the leaks.
You've felt the droughts.
You've survived the flood.

Now let's build the faucet.

Let's discover how purpose, pressure, and people form the blueprint for sustainable, multiplying leadership.

Turn the page.

The blueprint is waiting.

PART II – THE BLUEPRINT:

HOW I STARTED BUILDING

A journey from survival to structure—

where leadership became less about

personality and more about purpose.

CHAPTER 9: The Interview That Changed Everything

I didn't know I was walking into a faucet. I just knew I was tired of leaking.

By the time I hit 20, the hustle had run dry.

For four years, I lived hour by hour, chasing money and momentum. My instinct for leadership and strategy helped me stay ahead, but nothing I acquired ever felt like it stayed. Everything poured out as fast as it came in. **I was surviving — not living.** And definitely not growing.

I was lucky enough to have a long-time friend whose mom let me stay at their place. I finally had a roof, but no income. No direction. Just stillness… and the consequences that come when you walk away from a lifestyle that once made you feel untouchable.

One day, my friend and his mom went out of town and left me with the car for emergencies. His girl had just started a job and needed a ride. Vegas heat, pregnant, no car — I called that an emergency. After I dropped her off, I asked if they were hiring. She said yes.

I didn't know it then, but that question was a faucet.
That ride was a shift. I went home and applied that same night.

The interview process was brutal. Two-hour bus ride in triple-digit heat. I threw on my stepfather's oversized dress shirt — wrapped it twice around my frame — and stashed my headphones and bus pass in the bushes.

I spent four hours doing typing tests, assessments, orientation, and on-the-spot interviews. But I showed up. And someone named Sheba — someone I'll never forget — hired me.

I had zero experience. But I had a presence. Hunger. A spark.

Day one of training, our site director, Linda, came in with that coach-like energy. The way she spoke lit something in me — reminded me of football, of locker rooms, of game day. That day, I saw a version of myself I hadn't seen in years. Not hustling. Not surviving. But building, creating.

For the first time in a long time, I felt like I belonged somewhere again.

And more importantly — like I could grow here.

At first, I was just happy to have a job with AC. I was charismatic. Good with people. I made the floor laugh, hit the top of the charts, made a name for myself.

But it was surface-level.

I had learned how to enjoy the rewards of leadership without carrying the weight of it.

That all changed when I met Mishay.

CHAPTER 10: My First Faucet

Before I learned how to lead others, someone had to teach me how to face myself—and her name was Mishay.

Mishay reminded me of my mom. No-nonsense, all substance. When everyone else praised my 90% Quality (QA) score, she asked why I didn't get 100%. When others laughed at my jokes, she called out my habits. She saw through me. And then she pulled me up.

She challenged me to use my skills for more than just performance. Gave me space to lead training huddles. Taught me how to break down data, share best practices, and influence results. She was the first one to say, *"Stop performing. Start leading."* That shook me.

But the moment that really changed me came one night when I had a choice.

I had just gotten a new car — three days in.

That night, I hit the Tropicana exit and had two options: turn right and head home to rest up for work, or turn left and go out with the crew.

I turned left.

Later that night, the car was totaled. No insurance. No doctor visit. I missed five days of work. Showed back up with a concussion, a knot on my head, and a bag full of excuses.

Mishay had already told me what was required to return to work after such an extensive leave. She'd made it clear. I didn't listen.

When I got there, she had me fill out an exit interview. No yelling. Just accountability. She looked me in the eye and said, *"You chose this."* And then she sent me home.

I'll never forget that bus ride. The same one I took to get hired… but now I was riding it in shame. I felt wronged at first. I was angry. I told myself, *"I got hurt, and they let me go for it."* But when I got home and looked in the mirror, I couldn't lie to myself anymore. It wasn't about that one night.

It was about the pattern.

The late arrivals. The shortcuts. The unspoken self-pity I carried like a badge. That day, I stopped seeing myself as a victim of circumstance and started seeing myself as the author of my choices. That was my first real faucet moment.

Not a job. Not a title. Not a check. Ownership.

That's when I stopped leaking.

That's when I realized:

You can't pour into others if your own cup has holes.

You can't lead anyone until you take full responsibility for yourself. And from that point on, I did. Looking back, I didn't just stumble into leadership—I grew into it.

It started with a second chance. After a difficult conversation with HR, Mishay called me the next day and let me know I could return to the floor—but with a final written warning. That six-month period became one of the most formative seasons of my early career. I knew I couldn't apply for any promotions until that final fell off my record, so I locked in. I made sacrifices. I doubled down on my attendance, my punctuality, and most of all—my consistency. For once, I wasn't just working to be seen.

I was working to be ready.

Mishay and I inherited a brand-new team. It was a mix of tenured agents, folks coming off of corrective action, and a few wild cards. From the outside, we didn't look like much. But inside? We had heart. And we had culture.

We named ourselves Technically Speaking—a name I'd written on a slip of paper and tossed into the voting pile during a team meeting. Everyone voted anonymously, and when mine was picked, it was this quiet affirmation that I was growing into a voice worth following.

There was a young woman on the team, an artist, who sketched a logo for us that looked uncannily like Jerry—one of our more reserved but brilliant teammates. Jerry was deeply analytical and not always the easiest to engage in group settings. But I saw something in him. I spent time with him, learned how he thought, and gave him space to contribute in ways that honored his strengths. He taught me just as much as I taught him.

That became the heartbeat of our team: shared expertise and shared leadership.

Our rhythm was tight. Tuesdays were for metric reviews and one-on-ones with Mishay. Wednesdays, we'd run call calibrations and team huddles. Thursdays, we started a tradition we called Purple Shirt Thursdays. Everyone wore purple—it started with just us, but by the end of the year, the whole site was doing it. Years later, people still wore purple even when they didn't know why. That's what culture does—it leaves a legacy long after the team dissolves.

Technically Speaking became the number one team on the floor—for seven months straight. But more than that, we became a proving ground. We were a team that bred other leaders. By the end of that run, Mishay was promoted to Process Improvement Manager. I was promoted to Team Lead. One of our agents became a trainer. Another went into quality. Another joined the support desk.

We rose together.

That experience taught me something foundational: when you elevate, you leave a vacancy. And if you've been pouring into your people the right way, someone is already ready to fill your shoes.

Mishay wasn't just a great partner—she was a mentor. She spent time prepping me for my Team Lead interview, helping me understand my milestones and contributions while setting long-term goals. **She challenged me, but she never made me feel small**. Her investment in me became the blueprint for how I'd invest in others. And most importantly, I learned the shift from personal performance to collective success.

As an agent, I thrived on competition. I wanted to be number one. But as a leader, I had to learn how to let others win. And not just let them—but teach them how to. When teammates beat my metrics, I didn't sulk—I celebrated. Because it meant I was doing my real job: creating an environment where others could succeed.

Technically Speaking, didn't just teach me how to lead—it showed me how to listen, how to build, and how to multiply.

It was the first time I understood what it meant to be the faucet.

CHAPTER 11: *Forged in Fire*

My official title was "coach," but what I stepped into was far more than that.

It was my first formal leadership role—on a campaign for a large gym establishment. I wasn't assigned to their flagship program though. I was placed on a sub-client account, a fitness tech company that specialized in early wearable tracking technology—think precursor to the Apple Watch. It was a new partnership, acquired during a larger deal, but it came with little structure, few expectations, and no Standard Operation Procedures (SOPs) in sight.

When I was brought onto the campaign, there was an operations manager leading the effort. But just thirty days into the launch, they left for another job. That sudden exit flipped everything. Within sixty days of my own promotion, I found myself not just coaching—but owning.

I inherited the campaign wholesale: quality, training, knowledge tools, retention, social media, even client interfacing. I was responsible for building the curriculum, designing the knowledge centers, and getting our agents trained and supported from the ground up. I had never run a business, but this felt close. **Sink or swim—and I chose to swim.**

What's wild is that I wasn't intimidated. Not because I had it all figured out. I didn't. But I came from a world where chaos wasn't new. Things not being in place? I grew up in that. Expectations shifting midstream? That was dinner table talk back in the day. So, when I found myself in this environment with moving targets and absent blueprints, I leaned into what I knew best: composure and hope.

My early advantage was buy-in. While my client wasn't fully sold on me yet, my floor was. I brought two agents with me from Technically Speaking, both trusted and sharp. They were early adopters, and they helped me build team culture fast. I'd walk the floor with the same optimism I had sold in tougher seasons—this time, fueled by real vision. Although I was just a "coach" on paper, my presence and floor buy-in left me feeling empowered.

But being empowered doesn't mean being ready.

That lesson came hard one day when I was tasked with securing a training room for a client calibration meeting. I checked with every campaign, tried every corner of the site, even partnered with the learning manager to troubleshoot. Still—nothing. Ten minutes before the meeting, I had to break the news to my Operation Manger (OM) at the time, Mike: no room. He was frustrated, disappointed, and embarrassed. So was I.

It didn't matter that I had tried everything. It didn't matter that the site was fully booked or that I was still new. In that moment, I learned a painful truth: people don't care about the loops you jumped through. They care about the outcome.

I took that L and turned it into action. Within weeks, I helped design and implement a new booking system for training and calibration rooms across the entire site. That failure planted the seed for a habit I still carry today—stay ahead. Anticipate. Prepare before the ask.

Mike was green himself—new to our organization, unfamiliar with our systems—but he recognized something in me. While he didn't always teach, he set high expectations and gave me space to figure it out. And I did. We didn't always connect personally, but I learned how to lead up, manage the relationship, and get things done regardless of personality differences. That's a skill that would serve me in every endeavor since.

On that campaign, I realized that the ability to stay calm under pressure wasn't just a personality trait—it was a leadership asset. And projecting that confidence, even when I was learning on the fly, gave others something to rally behind.

This was my "forged in fire" moment. I wasn't just getting promoted—I was being prepared. Not just for more scope, but for more weight. The pressure I felt wasn't to prove myself to others—it was to protect what I was building. A culture. A system. A team. A faucet.

And in the fire, I started to see signs of water.

Chapter 12: Success without inclusion is still failure

I spent so much time under the spotlight—I didn't realize it was blinding the people beside me.

For a year, I had been winning. Eleven straight months of representing my campaign as the top Supervisor —month after month, my name was called, the certificate handed, the photo snapped, the luncheon with senior leadership booked. I had become a staple of what leadership was supposed to look like. Other campaigns were sending team leads my way to learn best practices. My one-pagers, talk tracks, and agent templates had started circulating the floor. I had become a voice in cross-campaign meetings—known for my consistency, insight, and energy.

I was proud of that. And I should have been. But something deeper was starting to stir.

Our campaign itself wasn't the top campaign. We were solid—middle of the pack on performance—but nothing that screamed excellence. My recognition wasn't coming from the collective success of our program, but from how I moved within it. My social media and tech support team, my quality and workforce analysts, back office department—each person I touched, I poured into. And they responded. They grew. They performed. They flourished.

But somewhere along the way, I forgot that leadership wasn't just about the people who reported to me.

I remember the moment it clicked. It was during the twelfth month of being named Director All-Star. That month, it came down to a tie between me and another leader. A peer I deeply respected. She had been working tirelessly that month—driving performance, locking in with her agents, showing visible growth and presence.

The tiebreaker came down to attrition. And I edged her out.

I remember the pride that welled up in me—twelve months straight. A full year! I had done it. I could already smell the prime rib and hear my name echoing in conversations around the table.

What I didn't realize until later was what that moment did to her. Not just the loss—but the way I celebrated it. The way I allowed it to be just another notch on my belt.

A moment of personal glory. Not team empowerment.

She never said anything directly. But I saw it. The drop in her morale the next month. The way the spark dimmed just a little. And it hurt, because I admired her. I respected her grind. And I missed the moment to amplify it.

That's when I realized something uncomfortable:

My success had become mine alone. I was finding the *"me" in "team"*, over and over again.

Leadership is supposed to multiply. It's supposed to reflect light, not absorb it all.

Yes, I was empowering my agents. Yes, I was pouring into the people directly under me. But I wasn't making space for the ones beside me. For the other leaders grinding, learning, growing.

And the truth is, sometimes the people you overlook are the ones who need your belief the most.

Looking back, I wonder how much more powerful that moment could have been if I had stepped aside. If I had used my platform to elevate someone else's effort instead of competing for one more accolade. If I had said, *"This month isn't about me. She deserves this one."*

There's a cost to constant success if you don't invite others into it.

People stop celebrating with you. They start resenting the system, or worse, questioning themselves. The room grows quiet when your name is called, not because they don't admire you—but because they don't see themselves in your win.

And that's not the kind of leader I wanted to be.

It was a sobering lesson: *Recognition doesn't mean you've arrived. It means you have more responsibility to reflect, include, and empower.*

That month taught me more than the eleven before it.

Because real success isn't about how long you hold the mic—it's about how many people you hand it to.

Chapter 13: The Pilot

Opportunity doesn't always knock—it whispers your name in rooms you didn't know you'd entered.

That's how the military insurance pilot came to me. I didn't apply. I didn't lobby. I was selected.

After a year of consistent recognition—twelve straight Director All-Star wins, a reputation for innovation and culture—my name started to carry weight in rooms I hadn't yet stepped into. When our company landed a pilot with a prestigious military insurance provider, they needed someone who could bring stability, leadership, and results. My name was at the top of the list.

Our previous director had transitioned out, and Cassidy was assigned to the site—a young, passionate leader known for maximizing talent in hot markets. His job was to bring the best out of us, and he saw something in me worth pouring into.

While I'll share more about Cassidy's impact in a later chapter, what mattered then was the door he opened. He promoted me to Operation Manager. Trusted me with the pilot. Stood behind me when others questioned if I was too young, too green, or too unconventional for a campaign this high-profile.

What I didn't realize at the time was that this opportunity wasn't about building a high-performing team—**it was about proving I could build leaders.**

The pilot was risky. High-visibility. High-stakes. In my previous campaign, being middle of the pack was acceptable—expected even. But this was different. This was sacred ground. This client carried weight internally. A successful pilot could unlock more business. A misstep would do more than cost us a contract—it would cost us trust and reputation.

It was a chance. And a test.

At first, I was afraid.

New culture. New expectations. New playbook. Everything felt watched. Measured. Graded. There was no space for "figuring it out as you go." But what we lacked in structure, we made up for in conviction.

Initially I had Abdul with me, a breakout star from my social media team. He was recently promoted to a team lead in training—bold, brash, outspoken—and exactly what I needed. Where I smoothed things over, he called things out. Where I brought calm and solutions, he brought urgency and fire. We balanced each other out. I took the PM shift, he held the AM. We'd tag-team our floor, texting each other real time updates on off days, and challenging agents to hold the line, to hold the standard.

It worked.

For the first time in my career, I wasn't just a standout on a struggling campaign—I was part of a winning one. And not just winning on paper, but in spirit. In culture.

There was something different behind that wall. You could feel it. The buy-in. The pride. The ownership. People weren't just showing up for a paycheck. They were showing up because they believed in the mission—and because they believed in us.

That belief was the true currency. It bought us time. Grace. Momentum.

We made mistakes, but we owned them. We had hard days, but we stayed in it. And slowly, that 30-person pilot started to grow.

At first as I mentioned, I thought I was being brought in to replicate what I'd done before—to build another great team. But I started to see, I was being called to something greater: To build other builders. To take people like Abdul and give them the tools, the exposure, the leadership voice to create change themselves.

And that's what leadership that multiplies really is.

Not shining alone—but building a stage big enough for others to shine too.

Chapter 14: When the Leaks Return

What happens when the faucet is flowing at work—but the pipes at home are bursting?

It's a question I didn't know I was living the answer to.

At work, I was forecasting six months out—building people, processes, and strategy. But in my personal life, I couldn't see past the week.

I was a new father, trying to transition from catching the bus to owning a car, from couch surfing to finally putting a roof over my family's head. I was constructing systems by day and confronting instability by night.

My finances were tight. My time was even tighter. And while I was pouring vision and structure into my teams, I was still living in a check-to-check mindset that left no margin to dream for myself.

It messes with your confidence—living in duality like that.

To walk into one world where your voice carries weight, your strategies land, and your leadership is trusted… and then return to another where you're counting coins for gas, trying to make meals stretch, praying rent doesn't go up.

And eventually, the cracks started to show.

Not in loud ways—at first. Just a missed alarm. A forgotten email. A client meeting I wasn't fully prepped for. I was still performing, still present. But I wasn't as sharp. Wasn't as grounded. The wear began to show in small, silent ways.

Those weren't just time management issues. They were early leaks—evidence of pressure building behind the scenes.

Because when your personal foundation is shaky, even success becomes heavy. You carry the weight of everything you've built—afraid that one wrong move might collapse it all.

The hardest part? No one knew. I was still the go-to. Still the energy in the room. Still the leader people leaned on. But I was running on reserves, pouring from a cup I hadn't filled in months. That's when I learned:

Duality will break you if you don't integrate it.

You can't keep thriving in one world while silently unraveling in the other.

The leaks I thought I'd patched were returning—not because I was weak, but because I hadn't yet learned to ask for water myself.

But I didn't just sit in the tension—I started to build my way out.

One of the first steps toward reclaiming stability was returning to something that had always moved me: *Music.*

A childhood friend and I decided to turn our passion into something real. We set out to open a recording studio in Las Vegas—a move that, at first glance, looked like a side hustle. But in truth, it was a declaration. A line in the sand that said: I will not just survive. I will build.

We searched for a space and found a building in downtown Las Vegas that hadn't been touched in over 20 years. It was dusty. Worn. Forgotten. But I saw potential—probably because I saw myself in it.

My dad agreed to help me and my business partner remodel the place. For the first time in years, we were side by side again. We'd already started mending things before then—slowly finding common ground—but the studio was different. It wasn't just conversation; it was collaboration.

He had once dreamed of owning a business too, and in helping me build mine, we weren't just renovating a space—we were rebuilding trust.

I negotiated the lease myself—$500 a month, a steal for the area. Pulling from lessons I'd learned watching NBA stars structure their contracts, I added a "player option" clause—giving us the right to renew at the same rate when the term ended. It might've seemed like a small detail, but for me, it was symbolic. I was no longer reacting to life—I was negotiating it.

I was applying my leadership lessons in real time: building systems, forecasting growth, creating structure where chaos used to live. The same principles I'd used to lead teams were now shaping my personal foundation.

Somewhere between soundproofing booths and reviewing budgets, it hit me—this wasn't duality anymore. It was an alignment.

Work wasn't just something I did to survive—it had become a blueprint for designing my future. The structure I built for others, I was finally building for myself.

And the moments shared with my Dad? They became more than business. They were legacy—quietly transferred, hand to hand.

For the first time, I stopped seeing my career and my personal life as two separate worlds. I realized the same faucet that poured into my team could pour into my dreams.
And that revelation—that was freedom.

It was the turning point: from surviving to shaping, from managing to creating.
And it's the lesson I've carried into every leader I've developed since—

You don't have to choose between building a career and building a life. If done right, one becomes the foundation for the other.

Chapter 15: A Seat at the Table

There are moments in life when something shifts—not around you, but within you.

Moments where doubt is replaced with clarity.

Where you stop asking if you belong... and start walking like you do.

For me, that moment happened at a dinner table.

We had just reached a milestone on the military insurance pilot. What began as a high-risk experiment had become a blueprint for scalable success. We didn't just hit performance—we earned trust. The client doubled down. Expansion was approved. We secured our own dedicated wing, a multi-state contract, and a seat at the future planning table.

To celebrate, the client invited our leadership team to dinner. This wasn't just a meal—it was a marker. One of those nights where legacy gets toasted, where new players become permanent.

The restaurant was high-end. White linen tables. Jazz pianist in the corner. Menus without prices. Everything about it whispered, You've arrived.

But I didn't feel like I had.

The night before, Cassidy mentioned the dress code: business formal. Jacket required. I didn't own one. And though I had been winning at work, this wasn't my world. I didn't grow up around rare steaks and quiet pianos. I wasn't used to rooms like that.

So I hustled to a local store after my shift, grabbed a blazer off the clearance rack, and did what I could.

When I got home, my mom—like she always did—showed up in just the right way.

She handed me a shirt: deep purple, with a shimmer that changed in the light. It wasn't designer, but it looked like royalty. She didn't say much. Just gave it to me with a quiet pride, like she knew what this moment meant. Like she was dressing me not just for dinner, but for destiny.

So I wore the shirt. Put on the jacket. And walked in.

Still self-conscious.

The table was full of executives in tailored suits and Rolexes. Ivy League stories, passport stamps, confidence born from structure. And then there was me—Vegas-raised, first-time Operation Manger, in a jacket bought twelve hours earlier.

And then the music changed.

The pianist, who had been quietly filling the room with soft instrumentals all night, shifted into a medley from my favorite childhood film. Maybe it was a coincidence. Maybe something more. But at that moment, I felt seen. Like the little boy in me who used to dream of more had just been reminded that this—this—was what he was dreaming of.

Then I spoke.

Not to impress. Not to perform. But from what I knew.

I shared how we mapped the customer journey from the lens of an enlisted soldier. How we rewrote quality scripts around emotional intelligence. How we ran huddles, coached our reps, elevated culture. I unpacked not just what we did—but why it worked.

And the table got quiet.

Not out of awkwardness—but focus.

They weren't listening to my title.

They weren't clocking the brand of my suit.

They were listening to me. My strategy. My insight. My leadership.

That night, I realized:

I wasn't borrowing that seat-I had earned it.

Not because I looked the part.

But because I had become the part.

That wasn't imposter syndrome. That was impact recognition.

And across town?

Another table had been built.

Just days earlier, we cut the ribbon on the recording studio. What was once a 20 year abandoned building—had turned into something alive, breathing, full of life. The ribbon cutting wasn't flashy. No media. No menu without prices. Just family. Friends. A dream realized.

So while the dinner represented professional affirmation…

The studio represented personal redemption.

One table proved I could take a seat-The other proved I could build one.

By then, life had shifted.

I had a nice car. A home I could afford.

A rhythm not built on survival—but on intention.

I wasn't just reacting to opportunity—I was creating it.

Applying what I'd learned in business to my own life. Bringing the same vision, systems, and culture-building from the office… into the world I was building outside of it.

The faucet wasn't just a metaphor anymore.

It was real. Flowing.

Because leadership isn't just about where you sit.

It's about what you build.

And I had built a table.

One my son could inherit.

One my mother could finally rest at.

One where others would eat—and rise

Pause & Pour: Part II Reflection Exercise

Before you turn the page, pause here.

You've watched me learn to lead, to fail, to rebuild, and to pour.

Now, look for your own reflection in this blueprint.

Write them out. Pray on them. Revisit them. Let them work on you.

1. **When did you first realize that surviving wasn't the same as living?**

    - *What old pattern had to break before growth began?*

2. **Who has been your *Mishay*—the person who saw your potential but refused to let your excuses protect it?**

    - *How did their correction shape your calling?*

3. **Think of a time you celebrated a win but missed the chance to include someone else in it.**

    - *What could that moment have looked like if you'd chosen collaboration over competition?*

4. **Where in your life are you still leading on empty—thriving publicly but leaking privately?**

   - *What would it take to build alignment instead of duality?*

5. **What "tables" have you been invited to sit at… and which ones are you being called to build?**

You've seen the pattern by now:

Leadership isn't luck. It's lineage. Every lesson leaves a blueprint—every failure, a foundation; every second chance, a stone. You don't have to have it all together to start building. You just have to be willing to build *honestly*.

Because the blueprint isn't about perfection. It's about becoming the kind of leader who pours, includes, and multiplies.

Before we move into the next part—*The Pour*—pause here.
The pages ahead aren't more story; they're a mirror.
Each question will help you trace your own leaks, your own blueprints, your own becoming.

You've seen how I built.
Now, let's see what's being built in you.

Turn the page.
Your reflection is waiting.

Part I & II Mid-Book

Reflection: *The Faucet in You*

You've journeyed through the leaks that shaped me and the blueprints that built me. You've watched me find structure, stumble in success, and learn how to lead from overflow instead of emptiness. But this book was never just about my story—*it was always reaching for yours.*

The pages that follow are mirrors, not recaps. Each question ties to a chapter you've already lived with me, **but its answer lives inside you.**

Take your time.

Write them out.

Pray through them.

Revisit them when the pressure returns.

These reflections aren't about reliving pain—they're about recognizing patterns. They remind you that leadership isn't built in titles, but in tension. That growth isn't found in comfort, but in correction. That somewhere between your leaks and your blueprint, a faucet is forming.

You don't need to have the "right answers", you just need to be honest enough to ask the questions.

So breathe. Grab a journal. And when you're ready—turn the page. The next section is waiting to show you how what you've built can begin to pour.

The Leaks

Chapter 1: Before you had words for it, what pressure did you learn to carry in silence?

Chapter 2: Where did you first learn to adapt instead of belong?

Chapter 3: Who built with bricks so you could dream in blueprints?

Chapter 4: What relationship have you misunderstood, because it didn't come in the form you needed?

Chapter 5: Which of your gifts was born out of being overlooked?

Chapter 6: What did you have to leave behind to be accepted in certain rooms?

Chapter 7: What pain have you learned to dress up in public, and what has it cost you?

Chapter 8: Who in your life has modeled what it means to handle pressure with grace, and what did their example teach you about your own response to pressure?

The Blueprint

Chapter 9: What consequence felt unfair, until you realized it was the result of your actions?

Chapter 10: What's a ripple you started that outlived your presence?

Chapter 11: Where are you trying hard—but still not hitting what matters most?

Chapter 12: What's one win you celebrated that someone else had to grieve?

Chapter 13: Who brings out the builder in you—by being their bold, authentic self?

Chapter 14: What part of your personal life is leaking while your professional life looks solid?

Chapter 15: What quiet moment reminded you that you were walking in answered prayer?

Some floods destroy, and some droughts redefine—but both will teach you who you are when the water is gone.

Look back at all you've endured. Every season that felt like it would drown you or dry you out was actually shaping you. It was training your spirit to lead from depth, not desperation. You were being built—not for survival, but for sustainability.

So take a moment to celebrate, to remember what you've overcome, and to recognize that you are standing here because you learned how to pour even when the well ran dry. Don't question your capacity now. You've already proven it.

The faucet is built.
Now, let's turn the handle.

Let the pour begin.

PART III – THE POUR

From pouring to producing —

when what once flowed from me began

multiplying through others.

CHAPTER 16: When the Faucet Pours

There's a difference between leading a team and shaping a culture. Between leading for results and cultivating a legacy.

I didn't feel the shift immediately.

At first, it was subtle—someone quoting something I'd once said in a meeting I wasn't in. A template I'd built showing up on a campaign I'd never touched. A manager referencing *"Card-style coaching"* like it was a method. But eventually, it became undeniable.

My leadership was scaling.

What started as a 30-person pilot had grown into a multi-site, multi-state operation. We were no longer proving ourselves. We had proven it. The faucet wasn't just flowing—it was flooding entire departments with belief, structure, and sustainability. And the greatest part? I wasn't the only one turning the valve.

Former agents were now supervisors. Supervisors were now operation managers. Folks who once rode the bus to work were showing off their first cars. People who had once confided in me about living in weeklies were sending me selfies from their new homes. And leaders who used to ask, *"Do you think I could ever do what you do?"* were now running campaigns of their own—some of them outperforming mine.

I had become what I once needed: a mentor, a multiplier, a maker of other makers.

One moment in particular stands out. A leader I had mentored—someone with early perception challenges and a few scars from the system—had aspirations of managing their own account one day. They asked me to mentor them through the process of growing . I gave them my time, my trust, and most importantly, the permission to be challenged.

They didn't just rise—they soared.

Not long after, they beat my campaign for top campaign of the month. When the announcement came through, I smiled. Not just because they won. But because they came to me afterward, emotional, and said, *"You saw me when I couldn't see myself. You gave me the right to believe in this. I wouldn't be here without that."*

That moment? That was it. That was when I knew this was bigger than performance. Bigger than scorecards or dashboards. I was witnessing lives transform—not just roles.

This was no longer about being the best leader in the room. It was about creating rooms full of leaders.

I was brought in at one point to help stabilize a different vertical—auto property insurance. We'd done well with the Claims Department, but this line was struggling. That's when I started seeing the ripple effect. The strategies I'd implemented elsewhere started taking root here, too. Staff who once sat under me now led side by side with me—some of them carrying the exact same frameworks we had once whiteboarded in breakrooms.

People who I had once taught how to read staffing reports were now building them from scratch. People who had never dreamed of leadership were now shaping teams, writing SOPs, mentoring others. And some didn't stay with our company—but they stayed with the mission. They reached out to tell me how what we built gave them the confidence to pursue dreams they'd buried.

I wasn't just watching people succeed—I was watching success duplicate.

Some days I'd walk the floor and see echoes of my voice in their huddles. I'd see call flows I created now embedded into training decks I never touched. I'd hear affirmations being spoken over new hires, the same ones I once used to hold shaky agents together during their first week.

That's what pouring looks like.

It's when you're no longer needed in the room… because the room reflects what you already poured into it.

CHAPTER 17: Permission to Pour

Every great pour begins with permission. Not the kind you ask for in words—but the kind that's earned in silence, through consistency, humility, and care. Before you can pour into someone, you have to be trusted with their becoming.

In the previous chapter, I spoke about a leader who trusted me—who let me speak into their process, stretch their perspective, and ultimately rise into a role where they thrived.

But what we don't talk about enough are the moments before the breakthrough.

The tension.

The resistance.

The uncomfortable conversations that don't come with a thank you—but with silence, side-eyes, or second-guessing.

We talk about mentorship like it's always welcomed. Like it's always celebrated.

It's not.

Sometimes, the truth gets met with defensiveness.

Sometimes, belief gets mistaken for criticism.

And sometimes, earning someone's trust means sitting with the sting of your own words and praying they see your intent.

This chapter is about that.

The in-between.

The space between potential and performance—where most people get stuck. Not because they can't grow, but because no one ever stayed long enough to challenge them with love.

This is what Permission to Pour really looks like.

And it starts—not with strategy—but with trust.

From day one, I saw the gap. But I didn't rush in. I didn't assume access. I knew that just because I had the title didn't mean I had their trust.

So I started slow.

Honest conversations. Intentional one-on-ones. Feedback delivered with care, not ego.

And eventually, I asked for something most leaders forget to ask:

Permission.

Permission to speak into the areas no one else was addressing.

Permission to challenge them—not just based on numbers, but based on the person they were becoming.

Permission to point out the blind spots they thought they were hiding.

They were a Team Lead when they came to me.

Not a peer. Not a rising star. A leader with all the drive in the world—but very little buy-in.

They weren't unqualified. Just unready.

They craved perfection—but didn't know how to invite people into the process.

Their team didn't feel led—they felt managed.

Their peers didn't feel partnered with—they felt dismissed.

Feedback sat heavy on their face. Their posture shifted when challenged.

And though they hit the numbers, they didn't have the influence to go further.

Their success wasn't scalable—because it wasn't shared.

At first, they didn't want to hear it. Their responses were polished. Their justifications were tight. They were used to being right—and being recognized for it.

But leadership isn't about being right. It's about being real. And real, isn't always pretty.

So I told them the truth.

I told them their posture was preventing progress.

That emotional intelligence was more powerful than technical knowledge.

That people don't follow results—they follow relationships.

It was uncomfortable. For them, and for me.

But I didn't challenge them because I wanted to be right.

I challenged them because I believed they could become more.

And eventually, they gave me what I needed most: *time*.

They showed up.

Not just to our check-ins—but to the feedback. To the growth. To the mirror I was holding up.

They started leading with presence, not performance.

They started going into rooms they'd once avoided, talking to peers they used to ignore, owning conversations instead of dodging them.

And I started seeing something shift.

They weren't just growing professionally—they were becoming more human. More grounded. More followable.

The breakthrough wasn't overnight. But it came. Quietly at first—then all at once.

They were tapped to lead a new high profile pilot. New wing. New building. Their own culture.

And they rose.

They didn't just manage—they multiplied. Their campaign outperformed mine. And when the announcement was made, they came to me with tears in their eyes—not because they beat me, but because they knew I helped build what made it possible.

They said:

"You saw me when I didn't even know what I was looking at.

You helped me get out of my own way.

I wouldn't be here without that."

That's when I knew:

Pouring into someone doesn't mean fixing them.

It means showing them the version of themselves that success requires—and walking with them until they meet it…

That relationship wasn't just a mentorship—it was a blueprint.

It reminded me of a moment I once had with one of my own mentors, Brian.

He walked into my office one day and said:

"Do you know the highest turnover position in our company?"

I paused-He didn't.

"Operations Manager," he said. — with a half-smirk that told me he already knew how it would land.

It sounded rough, almost condescending at first.

But his tone wasn't careless. **It was calculated**.

He wasn't trying to embarrass me—he was trying to awaken me.

That smirk wasn't arrogance. It was intentional.

A look of someone who had **seen too many leaders burn out pretending they were fine**, and decided to challenge me before I became one of them.

"Let's pull up your deck. Let's go over your performance.

Let's make sure you're not one of them."

No warm-up. No fluff. Just facts.

I remember feeling small—but also sharper. Like someone had finally told me the truth loud enough to hear it over my own excuses.

That day taught me that **transparency is a gift—if you're strong enough to receive it**.

And it became the method I used to pour into others.

I didn't give people what felt good.

I gave them what helped.

That leader wasn't the only one I poured into—but they were one of the first who taught me what real trust looks like:

Not silence.

Not obedience.

But the willingness to let someone in—and let their challenge shape you.

That's what Permission to Pour is about.

It's not what you say.

It's the space someone gives you to say it.

It's what you build when someone trusts you enough to let you help them tear down what's in the way.

And if you steward that permission well?

You don't just build a leader.

You build someone who builds leaders, too.

Take a moment and ask yourself.

1. *Who have you been called to lead—but haven't asked for permission to challenge?*
2. *What hard truth did someone once tell you that shaped your growth?*
3. *Do you lead with clarity, care—and the trust it takes to be received?*

CHAPTER 18: From Shadow to Source

There's a part of leadership no one prepares you for: The moment when you're no longer the "rising star" or the "one to watch"— You're the one they're watching.

The moment when you look up and realize the people you used to ask for advice… Now look to you for answers.

It's not imposter syndrome.

It's not ego.

It's just… **arrival**.

And what no one tells you is that **arrival changes everything**.

Because when you're the underdog, everyone roots for you.

But when you're established—when the wins start stacking and your seat at the table becomes permanent—the dynamic shifts.

Especially with peers. Especially with people who once poured into you.

That shift hit me hardest with someone who felt like a big brother in the beginning.

We'll call him **Marcus**.

When I first met Marcus, I had more tenure in the company, but he had more life experience. He had served in the Navy, and traveled the world. Lived stories I hadn't even imagined yet. We formed a natural bond—one that wasn't based on hierarchy, but respect.

He taught me about life—credit, travel, financial wisdom, how to handle money with longevity in mind. I taught him about the business. He let me explain systems, performance, and culture—he listened in a way that empowered me, even when I was still figuring things out.

There was no ego in our exchange. Just mutual value. Just growth.

For years, that relationship stayed rooted in that balance. We'd talk about everything—our teams, our families, our frustrations, our dreams. He was one of the few people I could be fully honest with—someone who understood both **the weight and the worth of leadership**.

But time has a way of changing roles.

And eventually, life brought us full circle.

His campaign was struggling. The program lacked structure. Engagement was low. Metrics were dropping fast. The leadership team had rotated multiple times, and Marcus, who had once been so full of clarity and confidence, now looked tired. Stretched. Disconnected.

I was assigned to help stabilize the operation.

And in doing so... **I inherited him**.

At first, we both tried to play it cool.

We tried to keep it like it was.

Tried to pretend the roles hadn't changed.

But they had.

I wasn't just a colleague anymore. I was the Director.

And he wasn't just a friend. He was a struggling leader under my care.

I didn't want to hurt the bond we had built.

But I also couldn't let that bond blind me.

Because leadership is about stewardship—not favoritism.

And the truth is, **when someone is no longer able to show up for the people they're responsible for, someone else has to.**

That *"someone else"* was me…

I sat with him in honest one-on-one meetings. We reviewed scorecards. Talked about agent feedback. Discussed strategy. I gave room for him to find his way back. But the truth was—it wasn't just metrics that were missing.

His mind wasn't in it anymore.

He wasn't building culture.

He wasn't driving ownership.

He wasn't pouring into his people.

And in a way, that was the hardest part to witness.

Not the numbers—but the drift.

He had stopped fighting for the role.

Stopped adjusting.

Stopped believing.

And eventually, I had to stop waiting…

Managing someone out of the business is never easy.

Doing it with someone you've shared life with? That's a different weight.

But I had to make a decision:

Protect the relationship… or protect the business.

And when I say *"the business,"* I don't mean the org chart. I mean the people.

The 250+ agents showing up every day expecting leadership.

The supervisors depending on clear direction.

The client trusting us to deliver.

The culture that we had worked so hard to build.

That's what I mean when I say the business—not logos and lanyards.

People.

And in that moment, I realized: **respect isn't about avoiding hard decisions-** It's about how you carry them.

So I gave Marcus the same thing he once gave me:

Respect. Transparency. Space to choose.

I didn't drag him. I didn't cut corners. I didn't let him coast either.

I held him accountable—not out of pride, but out of honor.

I challenged him:

Either re-engage fully, or accept that it might be time to move on.

And to his credit—he did.

He exited gracefully. No drama. No burnt bridges.

And I'll never forget the last conversation we had before he left.

He said, *"You did the right thing. I wasn't there anymore. But I appreciate that you were."*

That moment taught me one of the most sobering truths about leadership:

Sometimes the kindest thing you can do is tell the truth with clarity.

Not to protect someone's feelings—but to protect their future.

To let them see what they've stopped seeing in themselves.

It also reminded me of the need to **manage your transparency**.

As a leader, your relationships with people matter deeply—but so does your responsibility to the role. And sometimes, those two things will conflict.

What keeps you grounded in those moments isn't authority—**it's clarity**.

Clarity about who you serve.

Clarity about what's at stake.

Clarity about who gets impacted if you choose comfort over accountability.

That clarity became my compass.

It's what helped me navigate the complexity of being both approachable and anchored.

Both relational and resolute.

Both grateful for what we had—and responsible for what I was building.

Take a moment and ask yourself.

1. Have you been avoiding a hard conversation because of a past connection?
2. What relationship in your leadership journey has required you to balance respect with responsibility?
3. Are you protecting people—or avoiding the cost of telling them the truth?

CHAPTER 19: Altitude

There's a moment in every journey when the climb turns into a view.

You don't always notice it right away, but one day you look up—and realize you're standing in the very place you once prayed to reach.

I've received a lot of awards over the years—

From clients.

From peers.

Even from local Government agencies.

But none of them landed quite like this one.

It started with a conversation.

My site director called to share some news:

Our site has been nominated as one of the **Top 3 Sites in North America.**

He told me he couldn't imagine attending the event without me.

> *"It's not just the campaign,"* he said. *"It's your impact. The influence you've had on the people. I know we're being honored—but I'm not going unless you're there too."*

That moment meant something.

Not because of the spotlight.

But because someone I respected saw my contribution—and said it out loud...

The event was in **Colombia**.

To attend, I needed something I'd never had before:

A passport.

For most people, that's paperwork.

For me, it was a personal milestone.

There was a time I couldn't afford to leave the state, let alone the country.

Now I was boarding a plane to represent a site I had helped build from scratch.

I remember looking out the airplane window and thinking back to my first client call—

The one that left me rattled, questioning everything, silent on the ride home.

That window once showed me doubt.

Now, it showed me altitude.

I wasn't on a private jet.

But I was **30,000 feet above the life I had once thought I'd be stuck in.**

Colombia wasn't just a trip—**it was a test of presence.**

At one of the sessions, I sat in a high-level breakout room surrounded by the organization's top leaders—our Chief Client Officer, our COO, our VP of Operations.

These weren't just names on emails anymore.

They were real, present, seated just feet away.

And for the first time in a long time,

I felt like the quiet one in the room.

I waited to be called on.

I felt the heat in my chest.

Ran through my talking points in my mind.

And when the moment finally came…

I spoke. Not with fluff. Not with flash.

Just with clarity. With truth. With earned experience.

They nodded. They listened.

And when the session ended,

they approached me—not just to acknowledge my ideas,

but to say they had been following my work.

Later that evening, the tension gave way to joy.

There was karaoke. Laughter. Unity.

I watched regional presidents and executives let loose, singing along like the walls had finally fallen.

But that wasn't the part that changed me.

What changed me was realizing I no longer had to prove I belonged.

 I just did.

That trip wasn't about the award.

It was about the arrival.

The teammates back home cheering us on.

The agents sending messages like,

> "Seeing you get on that plane gave me hope."

The colleagues I met who asked to download my playbooks, my philosophies, my frameworks.

They didn't just see me.

They saw what was possible.

We had built something that mattered.

And now, the world saw it too.

Take a moment and ask yourself:

1. Sometimes the rooms we fear walking into are the ones that confirm we were built for them all along. What rooms are you afraid of entering?

CHAPTER 20: *When the World Tilted*

I'll never forget the day the world stopped moving, but everything in me had to keep going.

You can build the right team.

You can build the right systems.

You can build momentum that seems unstoppable.

But what happens when the world tilts overnight?

COVID wasn't just a health crisis. It was a business reckoning.

And for me, it came with the weight of one of the most sobering lessons in leadership I've ever lived through...

Winning at all costs... comes with a cost.

When the pandemic hit, our organization—like many others—scrambled to adapt.

Protocols shifted. Staffing models flexed. We were still showing up, still building, still winning.

But in a climate of chaos, **corners get tempting.**

And the push to survive can cloud the need to slow down and see.

Some contractual nuances—especially around facility security and compliance—were overlooked.

Not maliciously.

Not recklessly.

But in that all-too-familiar fog of urgency.

As the senior leader, I wasn't the one who made the oversight.

But I was the one accountable for it.

I had a choice:

Point fingers, name names... or take the fall.

I chose the latter.

Because if you wear the crown when things go right, you've got to carry the weight when they don't.

I didn't exit in shame.

I exited in ownership.

That experience didn't tarnish me—it **tempered** me.

It reminded me that **no matter how chaotic the world gets, integrity doesn't get to hide.**

And what I learned from that season?

It wasn't just about avoiding future blind spots.

It was about understanding why they happen in the first place.

The truth is: culture is a mirror.

And if you glorify output without process...

If you preach performance without pause...

If you reward the wins without inspecting how they were achieved...

Eventually, it catches up.

And in that moment, **it caught up to us.**

I've said this before, but it's worth repeating here:

Leadership isn't about being the smartest in the room.

It's about being the most responsible.

The world was spinning.

But I planted my feet, took the hit, and kept my character intact.

And funny enough... while one door was closing, another was quietly opening.

A client I had once partnered with had seen my work firsthand.

They didn't just know my performance—they knew my character.

And when they saw that I was available, **they didn't see me as someone who failed.**

They saw someone who had faced fire and kept his foundation.

They brought me in—not as an up-and-comer, but as **a builder.**

Someone who had built before.

Someone who could build again.

This time, though, the landscape looked different.

The office was virtual. The trust had to be earned remotely.

The stakes were just as high—but the tools were all new.

I wasn't just restarting.

I was rebuilding—with more wisdom, more intention, and more clarity than ever before.

Take a moment and ask yourself.

1. *Would you take the fall for something you didn't cause—if it meant protecting the culture you helped build?*

True leadership carries the weight even when it's not the source.

2. *Have you ever won in a way that made you question what you sacrificed to get there?*

Not every victory is worth the cost.

3. *What does your integrity look like under pressure?*

Because titles impress—but character reveals.

CHAPTER 21: Rebuilding from the Ground Up

There's beauty in the silence.

For the first time in over a decade, I wasn't rushing between meetings, site tours, or calls. The pandemic had slowed everything—and in that stillness, something surprising happened:

I caught up with myself.

Ten years of grinding had flown by, one step at a time, one campaign at a time, one fire at a time. But now, for the first time, I had space to reflect—not just on how far I'd come, but on how I wanted to lead moving forward.

Up until that point, I hadn't always been intentional. I had been a recipient of opportunity, yes—but not always a seeker of alignment.

That silence helped me shift from accidental growth... to intentional pursuit.

A few offers were on the table, but none felt right—until I got a call from a former client. He'd recently joined a new company, one with a presence in Las Vegas. They were looking for steady leadership—someone who could help navigate COVID's chaos across multiple micro-accounts.

This wasn't a 500-person campaign. It wasn't a sprawling multi-state campaign. These were smaller accounts, under 50 FTEs each, spread across industries: airlines, smart home tech, e-commerce. And for the first time, the role was **100% virtual.**

That mattered more than I can explain.

Like many leaders, I'd paid the price of ambition. I'd missed birthdays. I'd worked 14-hour days, six days a week. I'd seen relationships strain under the weight of my dreams. But during the pandemic, I'd made a quiet vow:

If I do this again, I'll do it differently.

I'd pursue balance. I'd be present. I'd still lead—but I'd lead without losing myself or my family.

This role gave me that chance.

And I took it with a new mindset.

Gone was the young up-and-comer trying to prove he belonged.

In his place stood a builder—someone who had succeeded, failed, grown, and returned with scars that had turned into strategy.

I approached this opportunity not just as a job, but as **a blueprint rewriter.**

The virtual model was new, but the mission was the same: build culture, drive results, and develop leaders. The difference now? I had to do it all through a screen.

And what I learned quickly was this:

Charisma doesn't travel through Wi-Fi. Consistency does.

In-person, I had been known for floor walks, spontaneous coaching, and long lunches with agents who needed an ear. But in a remote world, I had to rebuild my presence digitally.

I had to learn how to make Slack feel like a side conversation.

How to make Zoom feel like eye contact.

How to make a Google Sheet feel like a coaching board.

It was uncomfortable at first—but growth always is.

There was **beauty in the reinvention.**

Because this time, I wasn't just pouring into people—I was pouring with wisdom.

I knew now that **inspection wasn't micromanagement; it was stewardship.**

I knew now that **trusting your team doesn't mean you stop checking the temperature.**

And I knew now that **process isn't something you teach when things go wrong—it's something you teach so they don't.**

With every call, I layered structure into the chaos.

With every touchpoint, I showed up as the same person—calm, credible, committed.

And with every campaign I touched, **I poured what I had once fought so hard to earn.**

There were early wins. My name carried weight.

People who had worked with me before vouched for my leadership, and that opened doors I hadn't even knocked on.

And as success started stacking, **I built systems that could stand—even when I wasn't in the room.**

But then came the challenge that would define this chapter…

and the challenge that would define the next one.

A notorious client. Demanding. Disruptive. Draining.

One that no one else wanted to deal with—because he expected more time and energy than his account seemed to warrant.

The directive was clear:

"*If you can manage this relationship—and we don't hear from him—you've succeeded.*"

What they didn't realize was that this "difficult" relationship…

would become the doorway to my next level.

Take a moment and ask yourself.

1. *What if the silence in your life isn't a pause… but an invitation?*
2. *What are you being called to rebuild—this time, with more intention?*

CHAPTER 22: *When the Veils Lift*

Every great partnership starts with honesty—but only if you're brave enough to go first.

For most of my career, I never had an issue speaking truth to power.

I was confident in my voice.

Confident in my team.

Confident in what I brought to the table.

But if I'm being honest—when it came to the client relationship?

There was always a veil.

I knew how to pour into my direct reports.

I knew how to align with my leaders.

But when it came to the client—I stayed guarded.

Not because I lacked the skill, but because **I didn't trust the dynamic.**

Too often in this industry, *"partnership"* can feel like performance.

A dance of pretending everything's fine while navigating tightropes of expectation.

So I played it safe.

I showed them the polished version.

Surface-level solutions. Decks. Margins. Performance.

And then I met **Ethan.**

From the jump, Ethan was... a lot.

He wasn't aggressive. He wasn't rude.

But he was **relentless.**

He asked questions that most clients wouldn't.

Pushed for clarity where others settled for comfort.

Rejected surface-level updates like they were insults to his intelligence.

At first, I was tempted to see him as difficult.

But over time, I saw the truth:

Ethan wasn't hard to deal with—he just refused to operate in the dark.

He had forged a strong bond with one of the team leads—someone who, frankly, had deep frustrations with our organization.

They had built an *"us vs. them"* bond that cast shadows of doubt over our ability to lead effectively.

So when I was brought in, I wasn't just managing operations.

I was managing a culture war.

One between belief and skepticism.

Between old wounds and new possibilities.

Between a client who wanted transparency... and an organization learning how to deliver it.

At first, our calls were short.

A daily touch base. Fifteen minutes. Then thirty.

Eventually... two, sometimes three-hour deep dives into the operation.

Not just what we were doing—but why.

What we were forecasting. What the customers were saying.

What we were hearing on the floor, and what it meant.

He didn't just want results.

He wanted reason.

And I'll admit—at first, I was defensive.

I felt like I was being interrogated.

But somewhere in those conversations, something shifted.

He wasn't trying to catch me slipping.

He was trying to understand.

And when I stopped trying to impress him—and started partnering with him—

The veil lifted.

For the first time in my career, **I saw the client not as a hurdle, but as a human.**

Ethan had goals.

He had pressure from his leadership.

He had something to prove, just like I did.

And the more I saw that, the more honest I became.

I started advocating not just for my team—but for his.

I helped him understand constraints we were up against.

And in return, **he showed me grace, patience, and curiosity.**

That relationship became **the blueprint for how I engaged with every client after.**

No more veils.

No more pretending.

Just people—on both sides—trying to succeed.

The trust we built wasn't just strategic. It was personal.

And eventually, Ethan extended an opportunity I never saw coming:

To join his company directly.

To build their customer experience infrastructure from scratch.

To architect the kind of culture we'd always talked about on those long calls.

It was surreal.

And for a kid who had grown up on the BPO side of the industry, **it felt like a rite of passage.**

I said yes.

Not because it was glamorous (*though the perks were nice*).

Not because I was trying to escape anything.

But because I believed in the work—and I believed in the why.

This wasn't about running accounts anymore.

It was about shaping systems, empowering people, and building something I could be proud of.

Looking back now, **Ethan gave me more than a job.**

He gave me **the courage to stop compartmentalizing my leadership.**

To show up fully—same voice, same values—whether I was speaking to an agent, an executive, or a client.

He helped me realize that **when you lead with truth, you never have to worry about playing a part. You just lead.**

Take a moment and ask yourself.

1. Where have I been holding back my full voice in relationships that matter?
2. Am I building partnerships—or just managing transactions?
3. What could happen if I trusted others enough to be fully transparent?

CHAPTER 23: From Contractor to Architect

Every builder reaches a moment when they stop taking instructions—and start drawing the blueprints.

That's where I found myself.

For most of my career, I had operated as a builder within someone else's structure. But this time—**I was the structure.**

This was the opportunity many leaders in BPO talk about:

The dream of being brought on internally by the client.

Not just as a vendor.

Not just as a partner.

But as a true architect of their future.

When the offer came from **Ethan**—the same client I had once viewed as a thorn in my side, now a trusted partner—it felt surreal.

He had seen my leadership under pressure.

He had seen the way I translated chaos into clarity.

He didn't want a consultant.

He wanted a builder. A leader. A partner.

And he trusted me enough to hand me the keys.

The offer came with everything I thought I wanted:

- A corporate card
- Weekly travel
- Headquarters visits in Silicon Valley
- The title
- The autonomy
- The chance to build something from scratch

And in many ways, **it was everything I wanted.**

But it was also **more than I knew how to carry—at least at first.**

The first few months were exhilarating.

Flying in on Sunday evenings. Out on Fridays.

My life became **airports and agendas.**

Client dinners and late-night whiteboard sessions.

Blueprints turned into action plans.

Action plans turned into systems.

I was responsible for building out:

- **Training:** From onboarding to upskilling—curriculums, assessments, roleplays
- **HR:** Policies, recruiting pipelines, payroll logistics, compliance procedures
- **Operations:** SOPs, escalation flows, KPI dashboards, workforce models

It was **full-stack leadership.**

And the wild part?

There were no departments to hand it off to.

I was the department.

That's when it hit me—**how much I had taken for granted in the Vendor *(BPO)* world.**

Back then, I had experts at my fingertips:

- Quality assurance analysts
- Workforce managers
- HR professionals
- Training specialists

Now? **I had to be all of them.**

Or at least build a version of them until we hired them.

And while it was overwhelming, it also reminded me of something I hadn't thought about in years:

How deeply I had studied each of those functions.

In my younger years, I asked questions most leaders didn't bother with.

I sat next to workforce managers during forecasting.

I spent time with QA reviewing rubrics.

I asked trainers why people struggled to retain knowledge.

I stayed late to watch HR process final pay.

I thanked the janitor.

I noticed how the room smelled after they didn't show.

It might've seemed obsessive back then...

Now, it was my lifeline.

One of the most unique dynamics of this season was my relationship with Ethan.

He wasn't just my boss—**he was a man going through something deeply personal.**

He was slowly losing his eyesight.

And while the job description never said personal assistant, I found myself helping with things outside the usual scope—reviewing emails, navigating reports, preparing executive summaries for board meetings, drafting operational strategies, and managing logistics for things like travel, hotel accommodations, and dinner reservations.

I was doing the job—his job—while also holding mine.

It created a closeness that was unprecedented.

And while the exposure was powerful—**sitting in boardrooms I wouldn't have entered otherwise**—it also blurred the lines in ways I didn't expect.

When you become someone's eyes, you start seeing the business through both their vision and your own.

That's when I realized...

This wasn't just about the business I was building.
It was about who I was becoming as I built it.

I was flying high—literally and figuratively.

But I was also breaking a promise.

The one I made to myself and my family back during COVID.

The one about work-life balance. About being present.

About not chasing so hard that I lose what matters.

And here I was again...

Gone five, six days a week.

Barely present for weekends.

Drained. Pulled. Drenched in performance.

Yes, it was rewarding.

Yes, it was next level.

But **it was consuming.**

And while I had the suit, the seat, the card, and the access—**what I didn't have anymore was margin.**

That part was creeping in. Slowly. Quietly.

And it would show itself in the chapters to come.

But for now, **I was the architect.**

The one trusted to bring blueprints to life.

And I was doing just that—with excellence, with exposure, and with everything I had to give.

Take a moment and ask yourself.

1. What foundations are you building right now—without realizing you'll have to live in them later?
2. What promises have you made to yourself that success keeps tempting you to break?
3. Are you still building from vision—or just from momentum?

Remember: Leadership isn't just about how well you build for others. It's about how intentionally you build for yourself

CHAPTER 24: Leading Through Discomfort

You don't really know what kind of leader you are until the room changes.

Until the smiles fade.

Until the tone shifts.

Until you're the only one in the room who can say something—and the only one who's afraid to.

Because what do you do...

when the person you once looked up to...

starts making the room hard to breathe in?

At first, everything was exhilarating.

I was entrusted with building something from the ground up—watching the ideas I'd once only carried in my mind start to come alive in front of me.

I was back in person. Back in motion. After the pause of the pandemic.

I was exploring new cities, connecting with new people, building relationships in corners of the world I'd never touched before.

I was sharing excitement with a team who was seeing their own growth in real time.

It felt like momentum. It felt like mission. It felt like reward.

But **culture isn't about how things feel when they're good.**

Culture is about what happens when pressure enters the room.

Ethan was under a lot of it.

The pressure of launching something great.

The pressure of losing his vision—literally.

The pressure of watching his own expectations slip through his fingers because what he saw in his mind wasn't showing up in the work fast enough.

At first, the signs were subtle.

A short fuse here.

An outburst there.

An inability to wait for systems or people to fully catch up.

And then... it cracked.

Delays in tools created impatience.

Team members felt rushed, unseen, or overwhelmed.

Commitments that other leaders had made weren't being kept.

Buy-in was slow. Support was fragmented.

But for those of us in the trenches, **the tension wasn't fragmented at all.**
It was felt. Daily.

And here's the thing:

Ethan's leadership challenges weren't always aimed at me.

If anything, I was in a position of favor.

I had his trust. I had his ear. I had his respect.

I had access... while others had anxiety.

I had freedom... while others were walking on eggshells.

And that's what made it hard.

Because now I was faced with the question every leader eventually has to answer:

Will you only protect the people above you... or will you speak up for the people around you?

Would I stay quiet because it wasn't directed at me?

Or would I advocate for the ones it was hitting hardest?

I chose the hard road.

The honest road.

I had the uncomfortable conversations.

I pointed out the cracks—not to shame, but to shield.

Not to expose, but to protect.

But it changed us.

Not in some dramatic fallout kind of way.

But in that unspoken shift where trust has to reconfigure itself.

Our relationship wasn't broken—but it was rearranged.

Because once you stand up to power, **the dynamic is never quite the same.**

And that's okay.

Because **leadership doesn't mean maintaining comfort.**

It means maintaining integrity—even if it costs you something.

There were moments when I missed the version of our relationship that was smooth, easy, in sync.

But I wouldn't trade the version of myself that emerged from those conversations.

Because what I've learned—over and over again—is that **doing things the right way doesn't just protect your reputation.**

It protects your soul.

Even when the world tilts.

Even when the room changes.

Even when the person you're protecting doesn't realize they need it.

You do the right thing anyway.

Take a moment and ask yourself.

1. Have I ever stayed silent because the discomfort wasn't mine?
2. What version of myself emerges when pressure shows up?
3. Am I building a culture that feels safe for others—or just one that works well for me?

CHAPTER 25: *Where the Faucet Leads*

Some leaders burn out when pressure rises.

Others rise with it.

When Ethan took a leave of absence to handle the personal and professional strain that had quietly snowballed, I didn't feel blindsided.

I felt grounded.

The truth was, the signs had been there.

His vision—both literally and figuratively—was clouding.

His health was declining.

His ability to balance ownership and delegation was thinning.

But the decision to step away?

That took strength.

That was leadership.

And that left me.

I didn't inherit a perfectly running machine.

I inherited transition.

Uncertainty.

A fractured culture.

But I also inherited **opportunity.**

The organization had just started building offshore.

We were moving into **Manila**—my first time ever launching a team internationally, not from the lens of a contractor, but as the representative of the actual company.

It was exhilarating.

There was a hunger in the Manila team that reminded me of the early BPO days: people who didn't just want a paycheck—they wanted a future.

They wanted a why.

And they showed up every day with a pride and gratitude that reminded me why I loved this work.

I wasn't just onboarding a team.

I was inheriting a purpose.

And then, in the middle of it all—while sitting poolside in Cancun, about to propose to the woman I love—I got the news.

The team we'd onboarded?

They'd been entirely offboarded.

And instead of panic or frustration...

I felt peace.

Because I knew—I had poured.

I had shown up.

Built something meaningful.

Laid the groundwork for someone else to pick up and carry.

And most importantly: **I had led.**

That moment in Mexico, on the edge of a new personal chapter, was a mirror:

You don't always get to control when a faucet gets shut off.

But you do get to control how fully you pour while it's running.

Returning home, I wrapped up my time with grace.

And before I could even start planning my next step, **the next step found me.**

A former director reached out.

He had heard I was available.

He had something he wanted to build in a region I'd never been.

The environment? Different.

The market? New.

But the challenge? Familiar.

It echoed the same hunger I had seen in Manila.

The same hunger I had lived through when BPO was just trying to prove it belonged.

Communities were being changed.

Jobs were transforming family legacies.

Systems were being trusted, not just tested.

And I wanted in.

Not just because I could do the work.

But because **I now understood what kind of leader I wanted to be while doing it.**

So much of my career was about **finding the faucet.**

But this moment?

This was about becoming it.

And with that realization came the transition.

From Part III: The Pour... to Part IV: The Practice.

Because it's not enough to have a story.

You've got to know how to pour it forward—

Into people.

Into process.

Into life.

CHAPTER 26: The Reflection in the Mirror

— a pause, a breath, a moment to reflect before the next verse unfolds.

We've come a long way.

From the earliest leaks of childhood pressure and inherited expectation...

To the blueprints of bold choices, relentless pursuit, and moments that built more than a career — they built character.

To the outpour — of wisdom, of responsibility, of leadership — in places that once wouldn't even let me in the room.

This book wasn't written just to tell a story.

It was written to honor one — and to hold space for yours, too.

Every chapter has been a window:

Into moments where I didn't have all the answers but chose to show up anyway.

Into leadership that wasn't always pretty, but was always present.

Into wins that felt like arrivals... and losses that revealed even more.

If you've made it this far, **my hope is that you've seen a bit of yourself in these pages.**

Not just the polished parts.

But the wrestles. The tensions. The almost. The rebuilds.

Because truth be told: **we don't need more highlight reels.**

We need more faucets.

People who are willing to take what they've been through and let it pour—

With integrity.

With courage.

With wisdom that's been earned.

We called this book *Where Is the Faucet?* because for too long, the world has obsessed over whether the glass is half empty or half full.

But I wanted to reframe the conversation.

What if the real question isn't about the glass at all?

What if it's about becoming the source — the one who pours?

What if the moments that tried to break you were actually shaping you?

What if the setbacks were just soil for deeper roots?

What if your story isn't just about what you survived...

But what you're now called to build?

So take a moment.

Breathe.

Honor your journey.

Honor the lessons.

Honor the weight you've carried — and the strength it's uncovered in you.

Pause.

Because what comes next?

It isn't theory.

It isn't inspiration.

It's practice.

In **Part IV**, we leave the story and enter the strategy.

We'll break down the systems, the frameworks, and the leadership philosophies that were forged in the fire.

We'll translate principles into patterns.

Reflection into rhythm.

And lessons into leadership you can apply in every room you walk into —

Whether it's the boardroom, the living room, or your own mind.

You've seen what it took to build me.

Now, let me show you how to build you.

Let's pour.

Part IV:

The Blueprint in Motion

Build like the leader you're becoming

depends on it —

because it does.

Chapter 27: From Story to System

By now, you've walked with me through the leaks, the lessons, the leadership, and the legacy.
You've seen the victories and the vulnerability.

But if this book ends with just inspiration, then we've missed the point.
Because **leadership is more than a moment—it's a method.**

Part IV is where we transition from narrative to blueprint.
This is where we pour—not just into the page—but **into your practice.**

Why Systems Matter

In the world of operations, we love playbooks—handbooks filled with policies, procedures, and protocols.
But what I'm offering here isn't corporate copy-paste.
It's a **soul-centered strategy** forged in real trenches, with real teams, through real adversity.

Every framework in this section was shaped by a simple question:
Where's the faucet?
(And am I building something that pours?)

Because systems aren't bureaucracy.
They're the cadence that creates flow.
Without them, leaders get stuck in silos—reacting task by task, spreadsheet by spreadsheet.
With them, leaders multiply impact, catch problems early, and build momentum that lasts.

From Cadence to Flow

Throughout my career, I've noticed the same pattern—new leaders, senior leaders, it doesn't matter.
Too often, they lead in fragments.
They work the problem in isolation instead of creating a rhythm.

We'd never let an agent take calls without a call flow—a clear path that keeps every conversation moving forward.
But leaders? Too often they run without one.

So the real question is: **what's your flow as a leader?**

When leaders lack cadence, they slip into reaction mode—always behind, always late to the problem.
But when you establish systems that create flow around your people, you stay ahead.
You see problems before they become crises.

You catch the shovel before the hole is dug.

My First Faucet System: Engagement

The first faucet system I built wasn't about metrics—it was about **engagement.**

I inherited a coaching tool that could track conversations, metrics, and behaviors.
But like many implementations, it sat in the background like optional homework: *"If we get to it, we get to it."*

So I invested the time to learn it inside out.
I built a dashboard that pulled the data dynamically:
- How many one-on-ones were happening each week
- Which leaders were meeting with their people—and which weren't
- What conversations were being held, and what metrics were being ignored

And to make the data meaningful, I created a **simple disposition code system** for every one-on-one: recognition, absenteeism, performance, or development.
This way, I could see not just how many conversations were happening—but *why* they were happening.
It moved the focus from counting meetings to **measuring intent.**

What used to take 10–15 hours of chasing down reports now took 30 minutes.

And then I made it visible.
We posted a visual board right on the floor:
- *"Today: 36 one-on-ones scheduled."*
- *"Yesterday: 45 completed."*
- Key team metrics right next to engagement counts.

Engagement wasn't invisible anymore. It became culture.

The Results of Flow

Here's what happened when leaders started walking with their people consistently:
- **Customer Satisfaction (CSAT):** +4.8% in six weeks
- **Quality Assurance (QA):** climbed by a sustainable 6%
- **Speed to Green (new hire ramp):** reduced by nearly two weeks
- **Attrition:** dropped by 3%, as leaders caught struggles early instead of waiting until people were six feet deep

The faucet worked because it shifted focus from chasing numbers to creating flow with people.

And when leaders consistently engaged their people, performance naturally turned around.

Catching the Shovel Early

Too often as leaders, we wait until the people we're leading are six feet deep before we step in—either to try to pull them out, or worse, to throw the dirt over them.

But when you walk alongside your people, you notice the moment they grab a shovel.
You see when they're headed back to the shed.
You recognize when they've just pressed the blade into the ground.
And because you're there, you can stop them from digging further.

Data will always show the problem late.
People will show you the problem early—if you have the cadence to walk beside them.

Celebrating the Right Wins

The final shift was what we celebrated.
If a leader was supposed to meet with 15 people that week and they did—*meaningfully*—that was the win we highlighted.

Because **when you celebrate engagement, performance follows.**
But when you only celebrate numbers, leaders chase reports and neglect people.

From Calendar to Cadence

This is the faucet mindset.
Your dashboard isn't just data—it's visibility.
Your systems aren't bureaucracy—they're **the faucet that multiplies leadership.**

And when you stop filling your calendar with tasks and start filling it with people, **you create true flow.**

Because when your story becomes a system, you no longer lead by accident.
You lead by design.

Principle:

Leadership isn't sustained by moments—it's multiplied by systems.

Practice:

Build your first faucet system around **engagement.**
Track meetings, disposition them for clarity, make them visible, and celebrate leaders who walk with their people.

Prompt:

If someone observed your leadership this week, would they see flow that keeps people moving forward—or fragments that leave you reacting behind?

A Quick Warning

None of these frameworks will work if you treat them as tools for your title alone.
They're meant to serve you as a human first—
a father, a mother, a partner, a creator.

The point isn't to become a more efficient machine.
It's to become a more aligned leader—
with less regret and more impact.

So if you've ever led a team, a family, or even yourself, **you're in the right place.**
Because **cracks in systems are often just reflections of cracks in culture—**
and that includes your own.

Chapter 28: The Leaks

You can't fix what you won't face.

You can't face what you don't feel.

And you'll never feel it if all you measure is metrics.

At the heart of every struggling team, lagging report, or stubborn pattern is something deeper—a leak.

That's the metaphor we've carried throughout this book. But here in Part IV, it becomes a model. Because while people often think performance is about numbers, the truth is:

Numbers only expose the symptoms—Behavior reveals the root.

Why Behavior Matters

In every ops meeting, sooner or later someone says it:

"Behavior drives metrics."

And it's true. But behavior doesn't happen in a vacuum. It's a reaction—a reflection of triggers, beliefs, and environments.

People don't underperform because they want to. They underperform because something beneath the surface is pulling them back.

Sometimes it's personal:

- A language barrier that causes hesitation to speak up.
- A background where education wasn't accessible, creating silent insecurity.
- A new leader is still learning how to navigate cultural cues.

Sometimes it's systemic:

- SOPs that are outdated.
- Workflows that favor the loudest, not the most capable.

- Unclear communication loops that feed misalignment.

Either way, the surface-level fix won't cut it. **You don't mop up a puddle while ignoring the pipe that's dripping.** You get under the sink. You identify the source.

You fix the leak.

The LEAK Framework

That's why I built the LEAK model—a way to stop patching problems on the surface and start fixing them at the root:

- **L – Locate the Leak.** Where is the issue showing up? What surface-level metric or behavior is signaling that something's wrong?

- **E – Examine the Environment.** Look at the conditions around it—arrival patterns, workflows, tools, culture, clarity, leadership.

- **A – Acknowledge the Anchor.** What's keeping this issue in place? A belief, a habit, a process, or a cultural barrier?

- **K – Kickstart the Shift.** What immediate step can you take to redirect behavior and create new outcomes?

Every outcome has a root. Every behavior has a why. Every leak has a source.

Case Study: The Military Insurance Leak

When I became operations manager for the military insurance claims department, the first leak became obvious on a staffing call.

Evenings and Saturday mornings were overwhelmed with calls. We were consistently short by 5–10 FTE in those windows, and service level was falling apart.

Eager to prove myself, I told the client I'd fix it in two to three weeks. My plan was simple—reassign a few schedules. But when I tried, nothing budged. That's when I discovered what **LEAK** really meant in practice.

Locate the Leak: The issue was clear. Service level failures clustered in evenings and Saturdays. No amount of midday staffing could fix it.

Examine the Environment: Partnering with the workforce, I studied arrival patterns. The story made sense in hindsight: customers filed claims before work, after work, and on Saturday mornings. During those times, headcount needs tripled—sometimes quadrupled. Midday? The phones were dead. We didn't have too few people overall—we had too few people when it mattered most.

Acknowledge the Anchor: The problem wasn't just scheduling. It was culture. On paper, split shifts were the perfect answer—agents could work mornings, leave mid-day, and return in the evening. Saturdays could finally be covered. But a split shift without buy-in would collapse. What anchored the leak wasn't the spreadsheet—it was the absence of leadership to carry the new rhythm.

Kickstart the Shift: We launched the split-shift model and placed a developing leader over the team who mirrored their rhythm, held meetings at their intervals, and built identity around the challenge. What looked like an inconvenience became a point of pride. People wanted to belong to the "split team" that solved the impossible problem.

The leak was fixed—not because of a clever schedule, but because leadership and culture carried the system forward.

The Results

Once the leak was addressed at the root, the system started flowing:

- *Service level* (evenings/weekends): *increased 10–15%.*
- *Saturday mornings*: *sustained +60% improvement.*
- *CSAT and QA*: *both climbed as wait times shrank*
- *Sustainability*: *the model held for years, because culture—not compliance—kept it flowing.*

The lesson was clear: spreadsheets can locate the leak, but only leaders can keep it flowing.

Remember: You Are the Plumber

The truth is, we all have leaks—professionally and personally. Teams have leaks. Systems have leaks.

Leaders themselves have leaks.

The question isn't if you'll face them.

The question is whether you'll get under the sink and fix them—or just mop around the puddles.

Professionally, **LEAK** has helped me solve performance challenges, staffing issues, and retention risks.

Personally, it's given me empathy.

Because once you stop treating underperformance as defiance and start seeing it as a signal, your **whole approach changes.**

- ☐ You ask questions differently.
- ☐ You lead with more patience.
- ☐ You reflect with more honesty.
- ☐ You stop trying to fix people—and start fixing environments so people can thrive.

That's the difference between a manager and a leader.

Managers patch holes—Leaders fix the system so it keeps flowing.

Take a Moment and Challenge Yourself

- **Behavioral Audit**
    - *Choose one direct report or peer and list a recent behavior that frustrated you. Ask yourself: What might this behavior be signaling? Don't assume—investigate.*
- **Environment Scan**
    - *Review one area of your team's workflow. Ask: Does the process set people up to succeed? If not, what small tweak could improve outcomes?*
- **Leak Inventory (Personal)**
    - *Identify one personal "leak" that keeps showing up in your leadership—impatience, avoidance, over-functioning. Use the LEAK model on yourself.*
- **Change the Question**
    - *For one week, replace "What's wrong with them?" with: "What haven't I asked yet?" Reflect on what shifts in your perspective.*
- **Host a Leak Talk**
    - *Introduce the LEAK framework to your team. Let them choose a system or outcome to analyze and solve together using this process.*

LEAK Framework Worksheet

Use this worksheet to identify and analyze the root cause of a recurring issue in your leadership, team, or personal life. Each section corresponds to a step in the LEAK Framework.

L – Locate the Leak

- What issue or pattern is showing up on the surface?
- What metrics, behaviors, or outcomes are signaling something is off?
- Describe how this issue impacts you or your team.

E – Examine the Environment

- What environmental factors may be contributing?
- Culture or morale?
- Communication gaps?
- Tools or systems?
- Clarity of expectations?
- List any relevant environmental influences.

A – Acknowledge the Anchor

- What belief, fear, or past experience might be anchoring this behavior?
- Is there a deeper emotional or psychological root to this issue?
- For yourself or others involved, what internal narrative might be at play?

K – Kickstart the Shift

- What immediate steps can be taken to address the root issue?
- What support, resources, or new habits are needed?
- How can the environment be adjusted to create a better outcome?
- Write one small action you'll take this week to begin the shift.

Chapter 29: Where Is the Faucet?

There comes a point in every leadership journey where identifying the problem isn't enough.

Yes—observation matters.
Yes—diagnosis is powerful.

But the leak is only the beginning.

The true work is in the fix.

You can spend months building a perfect case for what's broken.
You can pull data, build decks, and deliver passionate speeches about what's not working.
But at some point, you must ask the more courageous question:
Where is the faucet?

Because the most transformative leaders I've met—whether in boardrooms or barbershops—share one trait: **they don't waste time arguing over whether something is broken. They invest their energy in building a solution.**

And that's what this chapter is about.
Not sitting in the pain of the leak...
But finding the faucet that will pour new life into it.

From Root Cause to Right Response

After you've worked through **LEAK**—after you've dug deep, examined the truth, acknowledged the anchors, and created clarity—**it's time to move.**
This is where **FAUCET** comes in.

FAUCET isn't just a clever acronym. **It's a philosophy.** A directional flow of action that keeps you from spinning in the same cycles of damage control.
Where **LEAK** was about discovery, **FAUCET** is about delivery.

Case Study: Turning Around Auto Property Insurance

When I took over an auto property insurance program, **it was leaking everywhere.**

Attrition was in the high teens. Licensing exam pass rates hovered around 40%. And because the industry was regulated, we couldn't just hire warm bodies—we needed licensed agents who could pass exams and be reciprocated across multiple states.

Most leaders would've diagnosed the leaks and stopped there.
But I had to ask: Where is the faucet?

Here's how **FAUCET** guided us:

F – Focus the Fix
We narrowed success to what actually mattered:
• Improve licensing pass rates
• Reduce attrition so those who passed stayed
• Build credibility so clients trusted us with more lines of business

A – Align the Actions
We attacked culture first so passers would want to stay. We implemented engagement cadence and coaching, and we upskilled trainers into true property & casualty experts and proctors.

U – Understand the Why
Pass rates and attrition were not just numbers—they were **confidence, stability, pride.** Our why was **retention with dignity**, not seat-filling.

C – Communicate with Clarity
We partnered with local testing agencies and created a **concierge** role to guide candidates through background checks, fingerprints, scheduling, deadlines—removing the tripwires.

E – Execute Relentlessly
No over-planning. We moved. We opened local pipelines, expanded retesting access, and leveraged agency proctors for a lean, fast, repeatable system.

T – Track and Tweak
We inspected every step: weekly pass rates, attrition, trainer and candidate feedback. **Tweaking became a lifestyle, not an exception.**

The Results

Within months, everything changed:
- **Licensing pass rates** jumped from ~40% to **~70%**
- **Attrition** dropped from high teens to **< 6%**
- **Culture** shifted—agents felt supported, trainers felt empowered, clients saw results
- **Credibility** expanded—opening doors to larger insurance clients across sectors

And the best part: **this wasn't my solution alone.** It was collective leadership—leaders using experience to identify leaks and build faucets that poured new life into the program.

Beyond the Boardroom

FAUCET isn't just a business model—it's a life model.
Long before large campaigns, I was moving step by step in under-resourced environments. Instead of focusing on surroundings, I built simple systems that moved me forward:

- **Focus:** Fix what I controlled—credit, discipline, daily habits
- **Align:** Cut distractions; aim time and money at stability
- **Understand:** Know the why—build a foundation for the future
- **Communicate:** Be honest with myself and others about the goal
- **Execute:** Start small—savings, consistency, repetition
- **Track/Tweak:** Inspect progress, celebrate wins, adjust setbacks

Those early steps created stability my kids now inherit. **Same principle:** don't sit in the leak—**turn on the faucet.**

Take a Moment and Challenge Yourself

Don't just identify your leaks. Fix them. This week:

- *Pick a recurring issue.*
    - *Choose one leak you've diagnosed a hundred times but never fixed.*

- *Run it through FAUCET.*
    - *Write each step:* ***Focus, Align, Understand, Communicate, Execute, Track.*** *No shortcuts.*

- *Act within 7 days.*
    - *Take one tangible step now. Don't wait for perfect—**start the pour.***

Because **your ideas aren't leadership until they're in motion**

FAUCET Framework Worksheet

Use this worksheet to move from identifying your leadership leaks to activating meaningful solutions. The FAUCET framework is designed to turn insight into action—strategically, sustainably, and with impact.

F – Focus the Fix

- *Define the true issue by separating root causes from surface symptoms.*
- *Envision what success looks like when the leak is fully resolved.*

A – Align the Actions

- *Identify the specific steps required to fix it.*
- *Ensure your people, time, and energy are aligned toward that goal—not distractions.*

U – Understand the Why

- *Clarify why this matters—to your values, mission, and long-term goals.*
- *Identify who will be impacted and how you'll bring them along.*

C – Communicate with Clarity

- *Make sure everyone understands what's being fixed and why.*
- *Set clear expectations, outcomes, and channels to reduce confusion.*

E – Execute Relentlessly

- *Take the first actionable step now and sustain momentum.*
- *Anticipate resistance or slowdowns—and plan your response early.*

T – Track and Tweak

- *Measure results and document lessons learned.*
- *Use feedback loops to continuously refine your process.*

Chapter 30: Resistance Isn't Rebellion

Leadership is 360.
It's not just top-down or bottom-up—**it's circular.**
You're constantly inviting, observing, guiding, adjusting. And sometimes? You're confronting resistance not from strangers, but from the very people you're trying to elevate.

That's where **trust** becomes your bridge.
Not just the trust you extend—**but the trust you earn.**

When I Was the Resistant One

I've coached leaders at every level—from brand-new agents to senior operations managers.
The easiest ones to coach? **The hungry. The humble. The hopeful.**
But the most important ones to coach? **The hardened.** The ones who've been burned. The ones who think they've figured it out. The ones who resist.

I know this firsthand—because once, I was the resistant one.

Earlier in this book, I mentioned a leader who walked into my campaign and asked a question that stopped me in my tracks:
"What's the highest turnover position here?"

At the time, I saw it as harsh, even intrusive. I felt like he was inserting himself into my business. What I didn't admit out loud was this: **I was afraid of what he might find.** Afraid I didn't have the right answers. So instead of embracing his presence, I resisted it.

But then I noticed the cues. These weren't drive-by inspections.
He was showing up at 6:30, 7:00 p.m.—long after he could've gone home.
He stayed because he cared. He pulled me aside, not to tear me down, but to show me how he invested in his own people.

I thought he was bragging when he shared the elaborate things he did with his team—food trucks, movie outings, creative incentives.
But really, he was setting a standard. He was teaching me that leadership invests in culture, not just spreadsheets. That recognition has to be **seen and felt**, not just emailed.

When I finally stopped leaning back and started leaning forward, everything shifted.
What started as resistance turned into brotherhood.
He reshaped how I view recognition, culture, and time investment.

He taught me: when you truly see potential in someone, **you don't back away at the first sign of resistance—you lean in further.**

The BRIDGE System

That experience helped me codify what I now call the **BRIDGE System**—how you move people, whether they're resisting or embracing, **without breaking trust.**

- **B – Build Relationships First.** He didn't start with criticism—he started with presence. Consistent, visible investment that built trust.
- **R – Recognize Pressure Points.** He saw the gaps in culture and engagement I couldn't yet see.
- **I – Invite Feedback Before Offering It.** He asked questions that forced me to reflect, instead of just giving me answers.
- **D – Document Everything.** Not paperwork—**patterns.** He kept showing up, modeling consistency until it stuck.
- **G – Grow Together, Not Apart.** He included me and other managers in outings—building community instead of silos.
- **E – Empower Through Accountability.** He made time—even when he didn't have it—and held me accountable to do the same for my people.

That's the bridge. And once you cross it with someone, **you owe it to them to carry accountability with care.**

Resistance Isn't Rebellion

That season taught me something vital: when someone pushes back, it doesn't always mean they're rebellious.
Sometimes it's **fear.**
Sometimes it's **fatigue.**
Sometimes it's **a mirror** they weren't ready to look into.

But when you show up with **consistency, curiosity, and courage,** resistance becomes **trust.**
And trust becomes **transformation.**

I didn't thank that leader at the moment.
But I've carried his lessons ever since—**and my teams have felt the impact.**

Take a Moment and Challenge Yourself

- **Observe First**
  - I*dentify one team member or peer you've only heard about through others. Spend a week observing their behaviors firsthand before offering feedback.*

- **Document With Intent**
  - T*rack 3 coaching conversations this week. For each one, note:*
    - *The behavior addressed*
    - *The method used (invite vs. instruct)*
    - *The follow-up step*

- **Shape Differently**
  - *Choose one resisting team member and one embracing team member. Draft a coaching approach for each that matches their posture.*

- **Audit Your Trust Account**
  - *Who trusts you most right now? Who might feel you only show up when there's a problem? Reinvest in relational equity with intentional presence.*

- **Bridge Building**
  - *Write your own BRIDGE plan for a peer you're struggling with. Where can you build relationship before demanding results?*

BRIDGE System Worksheet

Use this worksheet to close the gap between where you are and where you're called to lead. The Bridge System helps you move from awareness to alignment—anchoring vision, values, and execution so your growth doesn't collapse under pressure but connects every part of your leadership journey.

B – Build Relationship First

- *Who on your team needs deeper rapport?*
- *What steps will you take this week to strengthen it?*

R – Recognize Pressure Points

- *What performance gaps or behaviors have you observed firsthand?*
- *Are these symptoms of deeper issues?*

I – Invite Feedback Before Offering It

- *When did you last ask this person for feedback?*
- *How might inviting their perspective shift your dynamic?*

D – Document Everything

- *How are you tracking coaching conversations now?*
- *How will you document the next three (intent, outcomes, follow-up)?*

G – Grow Together, Not Apart

- *What shared goals can you highlight to create mutual accountability?*
- *How can you frame growth as a joint effort?*

E – Empower Through Accountability

- *What follow-up structures are in place?*
- *How will you balance accountability with encouragement?*

Chapter 31: Self-Calibrating the Container

There was a season in my career when everything looked like it was flowing.
I was flying city to city for a growing organization—corporate cards in hand, hotels booked, campaign launches rolling. At the same time, one of my personal business ventures was thriving. We were being recognized, celebrated, standing on stages. At home, my children were growing, and my family was expanding.

From the outside, I had it all. Success at work. Success in business. A family I loved.
But I remember one night when the cracks in my container showed.
We had a public celebration for one of my businesses. It should have been a highlight moment. But my flight that day got delayed, and by the time I landed, the time with my family had already been cut short. I rushed from the airport to the event, arriving late, tired, and already stretched thin.

On stage, the applause was loud. But when I looked around, none of my family was there. I drove home that night with the sinking realization: I was everywhere, and yet I wasn't fully anywhere.

I had just enough energy to keep showing up—at work, at home, for my ventures, for my teams—but not enough to invest in myself. My rhythm was survival, not sustainability. And somewhere along the way, my "faucet mindset" had turned into a defense mechanism: pouring into everyone else so I didn't have to face how empty I was.

That night reframed everything. I realized that if I didn't learn to calibrate myself, my success would always sour.

Because a faucet is only as good as the source it flows from.

You Can't Pour What You Haven't Filtered

Leadership is not just about vision and execution—it's about alignment. And alignment starts within.
We often teach leaders to self-assess their teams, their output, their metrics. But rarely do we

teach leaders to assess themselves.
- What are you leading from?
- What's fueling you?
- What's draining you?
- What unresolved weight is bleeding into your decisions?

I had to face the truth that my presence on stage didn't match my presence in silence. My words weren't the problem—my source was.

That's when I began practicing what I now call the C.L.E.A.R. self-check—a framework that helped me stop leaking fatigue into my leadership and start leading from fullness again.

The C.L.E.A.R. Self-Check

C.L.E.A.R. = Center, Listen, Evaluate, Align, Recommit

Whether weekly, monthly, or even daily, this process helps me recalibrate and make sure I'm not unknowingly leading from a fractured foundation.

C — Center Yourself

Before you fix anything, center yourself. Breathe. Pray. Get still.
Leadership can't function well in chaos. Sometimes it's not the strategy that's off—it's your spirit.

Ask:
- What am I feeling right now?
- Where do I feel off-center?
- What's clouding my vision?

Centering grounds you in your identity and values.

L — Listen to Your Life

Your life is always speaking. The question is: are you listening?
Look at your habits. Your relationships. Your inner talk.

Ask:
- Where am I ignoring warning signs?
- What has my energy been drawn to lately—healthy or not?
- Are my relationships being nurtured or neglected?

Listening allows you to intercept small leaks before they become failures.

E — Evaluate Honestly

Get real with yourself. Not with shame—but with honesty.
Ask:
- What's working?
- What's draining me?
- Where am I not living in alignment with my values?

This is the mirror moment. The bravest leaders are the ones willing to look into it.

A — Align Your Actions

Reflection without correction changes nothing.

Ask:
- Where do my actions not match who I say I am?
- What conversation am I avoiding that would bring clarity?
- What expectations or boundaries need to be reset?

Alignment is the bridge between reflection and impact.

R — Recommit with Intention

Once you've centered, listened, evaluated, and aligned—it's time to recommit.
Not just to the job. To the journey.
Ask:
- What one thing will I do this week to protect my peace?
- Who will I reach out to for accountability or encouragement?
- How will I know I'm leading from fullness, not fatigue?

Recommitment isn't about perfection. It's about presence.

When the Source Is Clear

When you lead from a clear source, people feel it.
Your words land differently.
Your presence steadies instead of stresses.
Your decisions reflect courage—not fear.
And your influence multiplies—because it flows from something real.
This chapter isn't the most glamorous. But it might be the most important.

Because if your goal is to be the faucet—to pour into others consistently and intentionally—don't just guard the source. Live from it. Drink from it. Stay connected to it.

A faucet is only as powerful as the source it flows from.

Take a Moment and Challenge Yourself

- **Create Your C.L.E.A.R. Ritual**
    - *Choose one day each week for a 15-minute self-check. Journal or voice note your answers.*
- **Ask for a Mirror**
    - *Invite one trusted peer, mentee, or family member to answer: "Where have you seen me off-center lately?" Reflect—don't defend.*
- **Audit Your Inputs**
    - *Look at what's feeding your mind, spirit, and body. What's fueling you? What's fatiguing you? Adjust accordingly.*
- **Set a Recommitment Reminder**
    - *Put a calendar notification in your phone: "Am I leading from fullness or fatigue?"*

C.L.E.A.R. Self-Check Worksheet

Use this worksheet to realign before you refine. The C.L.E.A.R. System is designed to help you check your capacity, leadership, emotions, alignment, and rhythm—so you can lead from fullness, not fatigue. Before you pour into others, pause long enough to see yourself clearly.

C — Center Yourself

- What am I feeling right now?
- Where do I feel off-center?
- What's clouding my vision or emotions?

L — Listen to Your Life

- What habits or patterns have I noticed lately?
- Where is my energy going—positively or negatively?
- Are there any warning signs I'm ignoring?

E — Evaluate Honestly

- What's working well in my leadership and life?
- What's draining me?
- Where am I out of alignment with my values?

A — Align Your Actions

- What adjustments do I need to make immediately?
- What conversation or decision am I avoiding?
- How can I better align my behavior with my beliefs?

R — Recommit with Intention

- What is one action I will take this week for alignment?
- Who will I invite into my accountability circle?
- How will I ensure I'm leading from fullness, not fatigue?

Chapter 32: The Living System

Leadership isn't just built in boardrooms—it's revealed on fields, in families, and anywhere people choose to show up with purpose.

When I first stepped into youth football coaching, I thought I was simply giving back. I loved the game. I had a passion for mentoring young boys. I wanted to pay forward the lessons that had shaped me. My mindset was: *this isn't corporate—this is community.*
What I didn't realize at the time was that I had walked straight into a living system.

At first, I thought my contribution would be passion plus mentorship. But as I observed more closely, I saw the director of the program operating like the best leaders I'd ever seen in a boardroom. He wasn't just running drills. He was running an organization.

The Ecosystem of a Team

On Saturday mornings, parents and spectators only saw the product: kids on the field, whistles blowing, touchdowns scored.
What they didn't see were the unseen systems:
- The logistics of making sure every boy had transportation to and from practice.
- The coordination of leaders so each unit ran in sync.
- The resources provided to every team mom so the kids were cared for off the field.
- The recognition, incentives, and culture-building to keep boys engaged and inspired.

And at the center of it all? A director who had once been a standout player, but had also lived the realities of adulthood—successes, setbacks, and lessons learned. Instead of chasing personal accolades, he poured himself into shaping the next generation. What started with a single age group grew into a full program, spanning ages 5 through 14, with nearly a decade of legacy behind it.

This wasn't just coaching. This was operations. This was leadership. This was a living system at work.

Leadership as Biology, Not Architecture

For years, I treated leadership like architecture—lay the foundation, build the structure, and keep everything upright through strategy and strength.

But watching this program in motion taught me something deeper: leadership is biology. It's alive. It breathes. It evolves. It responds to what it's fed.

You don't just design it once and leave it. You nurture it day after day, practice after practice, season after season.
That's why leadership systems can't be static. They aren't machines. They're ecosystems.

What a Living System Requires

What I saw in youth football mirrored what I'd seen in corporate settings. The principles were the same:
- **Attention.** Every boy mattered. Every coach mattered. Every detail mattered. Leaders paid attention not just to plays, but to moods, energy, and whether a kid's shoes even fit.
- **Intention.** Nothing happened by accident. From parent communication to team culture, choices were made to build more than athletes—they built men of character.
- **Adaptation.** What worked one season might not work the next. Rosters changed. Age groups expanded. Resources stretched. The system flexed instead of breaking.
- **Accountability.** Just like cells in a body, every person has a role. When one unit slipped, another picked it up. When someone overcompensated, it was addressed with clarity, not shame.

This is the rhythm of a living system.

From Fixing What's Broken to Feeding What's Healthy

In corporate life, we often focus on fixing what's broken. But in football—and in leadership—the better question is: *what needs nourishment?*

When a kid was falling behind, it wasn't about punishment. It was about feeding his confidence.
When a coach struggled, it wasn't about replacing him. It was about equipping him.
When parents were disengaged, it wasn't about blame. It was about drawing them back into the mission.

The lesson hit me hard: you don't lead a system—you live inside of one.
Your voice, your presence, your decisions—they all create the climate. And just like a garden, it doesn't grow just because you planted it. It grows because you keep showing up to water it.

Becoming the Operator of Your Own System

Ask yourself: *What are you the operator of right now?*
Maybe it's a business unit. Maybe it's a football team. Maybe it's your household. Maybe it's simply yourself.

Whatever the scope, the principle is the same: systems don't just belong in boardrooms. They belong wherever life is being led.

Because every one of us is operating something. And whether we realize it or not, the health of that system depends on how we steward it.

Attention. Intention. Adaptation. Accountability. These aren't just leadership principles. They're life principles.
- **Attention:** Do you notice your child's mood before it becomes misbehavior? Do you notice your own fatigue before it bleeds into your tone?
- **Intention:** Are you shaping your family rhythms with purpose—or just reacting to the chaos of the calendar?
- **Adaptation:** When life shifts—finances, relationships, health—are you flexible enough to adjust, or are you clinging to methods that no longer work?
- **Accountability:** Who speaks into your blind spots? Who reminds you of your values when you drift? Are you empowering others in your circle to play their part?

In other words: you are the operations manager of your own life.
And just like any living system, your life needs rhythm. It needs nourishment. It needs honest feedback. Because what you neglect will eventually show up—and what you nurture will eventually grow.

> "A system is only as strong as the operator who chooses to live inside it."

Take a Moment and Challenge Yourself

Ask yourself:
- *What in your system is just surviving that should be sunset?*
- *What's thriving that needs more of your attention?*
- *Have you created a culture that encourages feedback from every level?*
- *Do you recognize and respond to signs of system strain early—or only after breakdown?*
- *Are you nourishing what's healthy—or just fixing what's broken?*

Now, build a weekly rhythm that includes:
- *A pulse check on culture (what are you sensing from your team?)*
- *A pattern review (what's working, what's repetitive, what's stalling?)*
- *A process audit (are systems still serving the mission?)*

You don't have to fix everything at once. But you do have to live inside what you've built.

Breathe into it.
Feed it.
Shape it.

Because leadership isn't a machine.
It's a body.

And every part matters.

The Living System Worksheet

Leadership isn't just about strategy—it's about systems that breathe, adapt, and evolve. Use this worksheet to reflect on your leadership system and determine what needs to be nourished, sunset, or restructured.

Pulse Check: Culture & Chemistry

1. What are you currently sensing from your team in terms of energy, morale, and motivation?

2. Are there any recent signs of misalignment or disconnection?

3. What is one way you can create space for open feedback this week?

Pattern Review: What's Working & What's Not

1. What are the repeat behaviors or outcomes you've noticed lately?

2. Which of those patterns are healthy? Which are harmful?

3. What small change can you test to interrupt a harmful pattern?

Process Audit: System & Structure Alignment

1. Are your current systems and meetings still serving the mission?

2. Where have processes become outdated or unnecessarily complex?

3. Who should you consult to get a clearer picture of system strain?

Leadership Challenge

- What in your system is surviving that should be sunset?
- What's thriving that needs more of your attention?
- Have you created a culture that encourages feedback from every level?
- Are you recognizing signs of strain early, or waiting until breakdown?
- Are you nourishing what's healthy—or just fixing what's broken?

Chapter 33: The Unfinished Climb

Success whispers, "You've arrived."

Discipline answers, "Keep climbing."

The danger of success is the delusion of arrival. It tricks you into thinking that because you've made it somewhere—you've made it everywhere. That the grind is over. That the growth is done. That the version of you who got here is enough to take you further.

But leadership—*true leadership*—isn't a destination. It's a discipline.
Whether you're navigating a boardroom or your own living room, sustained development is the difference between peaking and pouring. Between getting stagnant and staying sharp. Because when you stop growing, you start coasting. And when you start coasting, you start declining.

Growth Is a Daily Decision

Sustained development is about one thing: intentionality.
It's not just about becoming a better leader for your company. It's about becoming a better person—on purpose.

It's about asking yourself, even after you've "made it":
- Am I still learning?
- Am I still leading with integrity?
- Am I still stretching myself?
- Am I still honest about my blind spots?

Because growth isn't always upward. Sometimes it's inward.

Fatherhood and the Mirror

There was a season in my life where I could have believed the climb was finished.
At work, I had built a reputation. Anything I touched was elevated. My name carried weight in rooms I walked into. My ventures outside of work were growing. My leadership brand was respected.

It would have been easy to coast. Easy to settle into the applause.
But then I'd look at my children.

And suddenly, the climb wasn't about me anymore. It was about paving a road they could run faster on. It was about nourishing their interests, creating platforms, shaping their perspective. It was about making sure they inherited not just my wins, but my wisdom.

Through fatherhood, I realized my true leadership wasn't measured only in high-performing teams—it was measured in a high-performing family, in a high-performing community.
And that's when it hit me: the climb never ends, because someone else is always watching your steps.

Leadership Isn't a Ladder—It's a Mirror

People think leadership is about climbing higher, managing more, making more. But the higher you go, the more your reflection becomes visible—both to others and to yourself.

In the boardroom, people may follow your title.
But in life, they'll follow your truth.
Your consistency. Your character. Your clarity.

And those things don't come from promotions. They come from doing the inner work, over and over again, even when nobody's watching.

The Fear of the Light

There's a line I once heard that stuck with me: *our greatest fear isn't that we are inadequate. It's that we are powerful beyond measure.*
It's not the darkness that scares us. It's the light—the weight of knowing we can shine brighter, live fuller, and impact deeper than we ever imagined.

Because if that's true, then the question becomes: what are we doing with it? Who needs us to keep climbing?

Maybe for you, it isn't children. Maybe it's a sibling who looks up to you. Maybe it's a friend who fell and needs your encouragement to rise again. Maybe it's someone who sees your life and finds courage for their own.

Either way, the responsibility is the same: **don't stop climbing.**

This Isn't About Status—It's About Staying Power

Life will keep evolving. So must you.
As soon as you start relying on what you used to know—without refreshing what you need to learn—you become irrelevant to the very people who once needed your leadership.

Whether it's a career transition, a new relationship, fatherhood, starting over in a new city, or wrestling with your faith, sustained development means one thing: you never stop leading yourself.

Arrival is a myth.
The climb is the legacy.

And the leaders worth remembering are the ones who kept going—not only for themselves, but for everyone who needed to see there was a way forward.

Take a Moment and Challenge Yourself

This week, take action—not theory.

- **Identify one area where you've plateaued (personal, professional, spiritual).**
  - *Write down one way to challenge yourself in that area.*
- **Ask two people—one at work, one in life—**
  - *"Where do you think I've stopped growing?" Listen without defending.*
- **Reflect on this:**
  - *Is my current version of success still aligned with my purpose—or did I settle?*

- **Choose one daily habit that would stretch you and commit to it for the next 7 days**

Chapter 34: Legacy Impact

Legacy isn't what you leave when you die.
It's what you pour while you're still alive.

It's the way people speak your name when you're not in the room.
It's the systems that keep serving others long after your hands have let go.
It's the culture, the confidence, the courage you instilled in others—so much so that they carry it forward, with or without you.

What Is Remembered

I used to think legacy was about being remembered.
But legacy is less about being remembered—and more about *what* is remembered.

When people reflect on their time with you, what lingers?
- Is it your wisdom?
- Your work ethic?
- The way you made people feel seen, capable, and worthy?
- Or is it the chaos, the missed opportunities, the burned bridges?

This chapter isn't here to guilt you. It's here to wake you up.
Because the truth is—whether we realize it or not—we're all building legacy every day.
The only question is what kind.

From Survival to Significance

Most of us start our journeys in survival mode.
We grind. We hustle. We build.
But eventually, we hit a wall—and that wall asks us:

"Are you just working... or are you building something that matters?"

As I've gotten older, I've realized something about my own story: legacy isn't only about the battles we inherit. It's about the fights we never had to fight—because someone before us already won them.

Neither of my parents knew their fathers. But they gave me something far greater than absence—they gave me presence. They gave me resilience. They gave me faith. They fought for things I never had to.

And because of that, my children will never face battles I didn't even know had already been settled.

That's legacy.
Not perfection. Not applause. Not recognition. But victories that ripple into the next generation.

The Compound Effect of Pouring Well

You don't build a legacy all at once.
It's built drop by drop. Decision by decision. Day by day.
- The time you spent coaching instead of correcting.
- The meeting where you listened deeper than usual.
- The call you returned when you were tired.
- The young person you encouraged who wasn't on your org chart.

Legacy is often invisible at first.
But just like erosion carves canyons, your daily discipline carves character—in others and in yourself.

Life Application: Beyond the Boardroom

Legacy isn't just for CEOs or authors or pastors.
- It's for the single mom showing up when no one claps.
- The teacher who stays late to tutor a struggling student.
- The father who breaks generational patterns and speaks life into his children.
- The neighbor who shows up with groceries when times are hard.

You don't need a platform to make an impact.
You just need intention.

And if you want to create a legacy that lasts, you've got to lead your life like it matters—because it does.

The Legacy You're Living

At this stage in the journey, you've been equipped with frameworks, principles, and reflections. But none of it matters if it doesn't show up in the life you live daily.

This chapter is an invitation to zoom out:
- What is the ripple effect of your presence?
- Are you building something that will outlast your title, your tenure, or even your time?

Because you are the faucet now.
You are the pourer.
And someone is drinking from the well you've dug—whether you know it or not.

The only question is whether the well you're digging is worth drinking from.

Take a Moment and Challenge Yourself

- **Define Your Legacy in One Sentence.**
    - *If you had to summarize your impact in 10 words or less, what would it be?*
- **Map Your Ripple Effect.**
    - *Identify three people in your personal or professional life you've influenced. What did you teach or model for them? Follow up with one of them this week.*
- **Legacy in Action.**
    - *Choose one small but consistent action that builds your legacy (e.g., weekly check-ins, affirming your kids daily, mentoring someone once a month) and commit to it for 30 days.*

You've Made It Here

You've made it here—through the leaks, the blueprint, the pour, and the system.
You've journeyed through childhood pressure and boardroom decisions.
You've stood in the cracks of broken leadership and became the faucet others needed.
You've examined legacy, accountability, resilience, and alignment.
Now, you stand at the edge of implementation.

From Reflection to Action

This book was never just a memoir.
It was a mirror.
A roadmap.
A challenge.

Because too often, leadership books speak to the title, but not to the person.
They give you structure, but not soul.
Strategies, but not stories.

This was written differently—on purpose.
It's a testimony, a toolkit, and a call to action.
You've learned that leadership isn't confined to the workplace.
It's in how you parent.
How you forgive.
How you prepare meals, pay bills, show up when no one's watching.

Leadership is in how you live.

The Pour Was Never Just About Work

You've heard me ask it over and over again:
"Where is the faucet?"
 But maybe now you understand what I was really asking:
- Where is the source of what pours into you?
- Where is your system of values, integrity, replenishment, and truth?
- Where are you pouring into others? And what is pouring out of you?

If you made it to this chapter, I'm willing to bet something inside of you knows:
You're the faucet.
You've been the faucet.
But being a faucet isn't about having all the answers—it's about being connected to the Source.

Because when the source runs dry, the faucet stops flowing.
So this chapter isn't about endings.
It's about staying connected.

Don't Stop Here

Don't let this book sit on a shelf and gather dust.
Apply what you've learned. Revisit the worksheets. Implement the frameworks.
- Use the **LEAK** model to identify root causes in your life and leadership.
- Use **FAUCET** to action plan with purpose.
- Use **CLEAR** to self-calibrate and maintain alignment.
- Use **BRIDGE** to coach others across resistance into trust.
- Use your legacy as a compass—what you build today determines what outlives you tomorrow.

This isn't the end of the pour. It's the beginning of the overflow.

Pause & Pour: The Next Pour Belongs to You

No one ever handed me a guidebook for leadership.

But I promised myself—if I ever found my faucet—I'd pour into others.

This book was that promise fulfilled.

And now I hand it to you.

Don't wait for permission.

Don't wait for perfection.

Start pouring. Right where you are.

Let your life be the leadership lesson.

Let your impact speak louder than your insecurities.

Because the faucet... is you.

Take a Moment and Challenge Yourself

1. **Build a Pour Plan.**
   a. Choose one area of life (family, team, community, faith, or health). Write down one habit, one principle, and one system you'll implement in the next 30 days to pour into it.
2. **Schedule Your Source Time.**
   a. Block 30–60 minutes weekly for personal recalibration—whether it's prayer, journaling, walking, therapy, reading, or silence. Protect it like your paycheck.
3. **Legacy Letter.**
   a. Write a short letter to someone who poured into you. Honor them. Thank them. If they're no longer living, write it anyway. If they are—send it.

Epilogue — The Final Pour

The Final Pour is not the end.
It's the beginning of your next season of intentional leadership.

So I ask you, one last time—
Where is your faucet?

When you close this book, don't close the story. Continue it.
The next chapter isn't written by me—it's written by you.

Somewhere in your life is a person waiting for your pour.
A child who needs your words.
A teammate who needs your belief.
A stranger who will one day say, *"Because of you, I didn't give up."*

You may never see the full ripple of your leadership.
But you will feel it every time you choose to show up,
every time you choose courage over comfort,
every time you choose to pour when it would've been easier to withhold.

The faucet isn't just a metaphor.
It's your calling.
Your responsibility.
Your invitation.

So don't stop here.
Don't shrink back.
Don't wait for perfect conditions.

Start pouring. Today. Right where you are.

And when the pressure rises—remember this truth:
The faucet doesn't run dry when it stays connected to the Source.

That's how your legacy will outlive you.
Not in titles. Not in trophies.
But in the lives of others who are refreshed because you kept pouring.

A Note of Thanks

Thank you.

Thank you for walking this journey with me—for choosing to step into my stories, my struggles, and my systems. Thank you for seeing yourself through my vulnerabilities, and for seeing me in them too.

Whether you bought this book or it was placed in your hands as a gift, the fact that you opened it, stayed with it, and gave your time to it is more meaningful than I can ever put into words.

For me, the greatest reward isn't the writing of these pages—it's knowing that somewhere, someone may feel what I once felt. That in your own battles, questions, or pressures, you might find yourself seen here. Not only seen, but strengthened. Not only strengthened, but empowered.

And here's the truth: with every page you turned, you gave that gift back to me.

You reminded me that this faucet I've spent my life searching for, protecting, and pouring from—was never wasted.

So I thank you, beyond measure.

Because by reading, you did more than finish a book.

You poured into me, too.

I'm living proof that the faucet can be found, and as you close these pages, I hope you realize:

You've been holding your own faucet all along.

Thank you for letting me share mine.

Thank you for finding yours.

"The question isn't whether the glass is half full or half empty.

*The real question is: **Where's the faucet?**"*

"There was a man sent from God whose name was John.

He came as a witness to testify concerning that light, so that through him all might believe.

He himself was not the light; he came only as a witness to the light.

The true light that gives light to everyone was coming into the world."

-John 1:6-9 (NIV)

About the Author

Christopher Card Jr. is a leadership architect, speaker, and operations strategist who believes true leadership isn't defined by titles—it's revealed through transformation.

From his early beginnings on the call center floor to leading multimillion-dollar operations across the U.S., Jamaica, and the Philippines, Christopher built a legacy of turning pressure into purpose and systems into culture. His signature "Faucet Framework" was born from one truth: the question isn't whether the glass is half full or half empty—it's Where's the Faucet?

Beyond corporate success, Christopher is a thriving entrepreneur and community activist whose ventures blend leadership, creativity, and impact. From building youth mentorship initiatives and nonprofit partnerships to launching business ventures that empower local talent, he has dedicated his life to pouring into people, purpose, and progress.

A devoted father, creative visionary, and faith-driven builder, Christopher continues to challenge others to lead from overflow—not exhaustion. Whether in boardrooms, classrooms, or communities, his mission remains the same: to help others discover their source, activate their flow, and become the faucet in every space they touch.

Stay Connected / Speaking + Consulting Inquiry

If this book spoke to you — challenged you, grew you, or reminded you of who you're becoming — I'd love to stay connected.

Speaking & Guest Teaching

I am available for:

- Conferences & summits
- Keynotes & leadership retreats
- Faith-based gatherings & men's events
- Workshops, panels & podcasts

Consulting & Coaching

I partner with:

- Organizations scaling leadership culture, process & systems
- Entrepreneurs, creatives & founders looking to build sustainably
- Leaders who want 1-on-1 accompaniment as they develop their "Pour"

Let's Build Together

- LinkedIn: *@ChrisCard*
- Instagram: *@whereisthefaucet*
- Tik Tok: *@wheresthefaucet*

Appendix

Build like the legacy you'll leave depends on it — because it does.

This appendix isn't just extra pages; it's your blueprint in motion. The tools, frameworks, and reflections here are designed to help you apply what you've read—turning principles into practice and insight into overflow. Every question, every system, every pause is an invitation to build the kind of leader who doesn't just find the faucet, but becomes it.

LEAK Framework Worksheet

Use this worksheet to identify and analyze the root cause of a recurring issue in your leadership, team, or personal life. Each section corresponds to a step in the LEAK Framework.

L – Locate the Leak

- What issue or pattern is showing up on the surface?
- What metrics, behaviors, or outcomes are signaling something is off?
- Describe how this issue impacts you or your team.

E – Examine the Environment

- What environmental factors may be contributing?
- Culture or morale?
- Communication gaps?
- Tools or systems?
- Clarity of expectations?
- List any relevant environmental influences.

A – Acknowledge the Anchor

- What belief, fear, or past experience might be anchoring this behavior?
- Is there a deeper emotional or psychological root to this issue?
- For yourself or others involved, what internal narrative might be at play?

K – Kickstart the Shift

- What immediate steps can be taken to address the root issue?
- What support, resources, or new habits are needed?
- How can the environment be adjusted to create a better outcome?
- Write one small action you'll take this week to begin the shift.

FAUCET Framework Worksheet

Use this worksheet to move from identifying your leadership leaks to activating meaningful solutions. The FAUCET framework is designed to turn insight into action—strategically, sustainably, and with impact.

F – Focus the Fix

- *Define the true issue by separating root causes from surface symptoms.*
- *Envision what success looks like when the leak is fully resolved.*

A – Align the Actions

- *Identify the specific steps required to fix it.*
- *Ensure your people, time, and energy are aligned toward that goal—not distractions.*

U – Understand the Why

- *Clarify why this matters—to your values, mission, and long-term goals.*
- *Identify who will be impacted and how you'll bring them along.*

C – Communicate with Clarity

- *Make sure everyone understands what's being fixed and why.*
- *Set clear expectations, outcomes, and channels to reduce confusion.*

E – Execute Relentlessly

- *Take the first actionable step now and sustain momentum.*
- *Anticipate resistance or slowdowns—and plan your response early.*

T – Track and Tweak

- *Measure results and document lessons learned.*
- *Use feedback loops to continuously refine your process.*

BRIDGE System Worksheet

Use this worksheet to close the gap between where you are and where you're called to lead. The Bridge System helps you move from awareness to alignment—anchoring vision, values, and execution so your growth doesn't collapse under pressure but connects every part of your leadership journey.

B – Build Relationship First

- Who on your team needs deeper rapport?
- What steps will you take this week to strengthen it?

R – Recognize Pressure Points

- What performance gaps or behaviors have you observed firsthand?
- Are these symptoms of deeper issues?

I – Invite Feedback Before Offering It

- When did you last ask this person for feedback?
- How might inviting their perspective shift your dynamic?

D – Document Everything

- How are you tracking coaching conversations now?
- How will you document the next three (intent, outcomes, follow-up)?

G – Grow Together, Not Apart

- What shared goals can you highlight to create mutual accountability?
- How can you frame growth as a joint effort?

E – Empower Through Accountability

- What follow-up structures are in place?
- How will you balance accountability with encouragement?

C.L.E.A.R. Self-Check Worksheet

Use this worksheet to realign before you refine. The C.L.E.A.R. System is designed to help you check your capacity, leadership, emotions, alignment, and rhythm—so you can lead from fullness, not fatigue. Before you pour into others, pause long enough to see yourself clearly.

C — Center Yourself

- What am I feeling right now?
- Where do I feel off-center?
- What's clouding my vision or emotions?

L — Listen to Your Life

- What habits or patterns have I noticed lately?
- Where is my energy going—positively or negatively?
- Are there any warning signs I'm ignoring?

E — Evaluate Honestly

- What's working well in my leadership and life?
- What's draining me?
- Where am I out of alignment with my values?

A — Align Your Actions

- What adjustments do I need to make immediately?
- What conversation or decision am I avoiding?
- How can I better align my behavior with my beliefs?

R — Recommit with Intention

- What is one action I will take this week for alignment?
- Who will invite into my accountability circle?

The Living System Worksheet

Leadership isn't just about strategy—it's about systems that breathe, adapt, and evolve. Use this worksheet to reflect on your leadership system and determine what needs to be nourished, sunset, or restructured.

Pulse Check: Culture & Chemistry

1. What are you currently sensing from your team in terms of energy, morale, and motivation?
2. Are there any recent signs of misalignment or disconnection?
3. What is one way you can create space for open feedback this week?

Pattern Review: What's Working & What's Not

1. What are the repeat behaviors or outcomes you've noticed lately?
2. Which of those patterns are healthy? Which are harmful?
3. What small change can you test to interrupt a harmful pattern?

Process Audit: System & Structure Alignment

1. Are your current systems and meetings still serving the mission?
2. Where have processes become outdated or unnecessarily complex?
3. Who should you consult to get a clearer picture of system strain?

Leadership Challenge

- What in your system is surviving that should be sunset?
- What's thriving that needs more of your attention?
- Have you created a culture that encourages feedback from every level?
- Are you recognizing signs of strain early, or waiting until breakdown?
- Are you nourishing what's healthy—or just fixing what's broken?

Operational & Leadership Glossary

AHT (Average Handle Time)

The average duration of a customer interaction—from the moment a call or chat begins until it's fully resolved. A key performance metric that measures both efficiency and process control.

BPO (Business Process Outsourcing)

The practice of contracting business operations or services to a third-party vendor. In your story, BPO represents the global workforce—people and performance across sites in the U.S., Jamaica, and the Philippines.

CSAT (Customer Satisfaction Score)

A common metric that measures customer happiness with a product, service, or interaction, usually through post-interaction surveys. A reflection of both process effectiveness and emotional intelligence in service.

FCR (First Call Resolution)

The percentage of customer issues resolved during the first contact. High FCR indicates effective training, empowered agents, and streamlined systems.

QA (Quality Assurance)

The process of monitoring and evaluating agent interactions to ensure compliance, accuracy, and customer satisfaction. QA drives consistency between what's said, what's done, and what's delivered.

Attrition

The rate at which employees voluntarily or involuntarily leave an organization. In leadership, attrition isn't just a number—it's a reflection of culture, engagement, and trust.

Engagement

The emotional and mental commitment employees bring to their work. Engaged employees don't just meet expectations—they contribute ideas, energy, and ownership to the mission.

NPS (Net Promoter Score)

A customer loyalty metric calculated by asking one key question: *"How likely are you to recommend us?"* It measures advocacy and experience rather than just satisfaction.

KPI (Key Performance Indicator)

A measurable goal that indicates success in a specific area—such as AHT, CSAT, or revenue. KPIs tell the story of progress, priorities, and performance alignment.

SL (Service Level)

The percentage of calls or interactions answered within a target timeframe. Service Level reflects operational balance between staffing, demand, and response quality.

WFM (Workforce Management)

The practice of forecasting, scheduling, and optimizing staff resources to meet business needs. In your book, WFM symbolizes both precision and adaptability—making sure people and performance stay aligned.

Escalation

When an issue is raised to a higher level of support or authority. In leadership, escalations test communication, empathy, and system design.

Coach/TL (Team Lead)

A frontline leader responsible for guiding, coaching, and supporting agents. Team Leads translate vision into daily execution—they are the bridge between leadership and the front line.

OM (Operations Manager)

A mid-level leader overseeing multiple teams, responsible for performance, culture, and client outcomes. The OM role represents both strategy and stewardship—the "faucet" between people and process.

LOB (Line of Business)

A specific department, client program, or business segment within an organization. Each LOB can have unique goals, metrics, and leadership needs.

Client Partner / Director

A senior leader who serves as the main liaison between the BPO and the client organization—responsible for strategy, trust, and growth.

Site / Nearshore / Offshore

Refers to the physical or virtual location of a BPO operation.

- **Onshore**: Same country as the client.

- **Nearshore**: Geographically close (e.g., Jamaica, Latin America).

- **Offshore**: Distant but cost-effective regions (e.g., the Philippines).

Calibration

A process where leaders, QA analysts, and clients align on performance standards and expectations to ensure fairness and consistency in evaluations.

Coaching Cadence

The intentional rhythm of feedback, one-on-ones, and development sessions that keep performance aligned with culture. Great leaders coach consistently—not reactively.

Span of Control

The number of direct reports a leader manages effectively. It's not just about headcount—it's about the capacity to connect, coach, and cultivate each person.

Retention

The ability to keep strong employees engaged and growing within the organization. High retention is the byproduct of high trust and authentic leadership.

Performance Management

A structured process for measuring, reviewing, and improving individual or team outcomes. In your context, it blends data with development—accountability with care.

Copyright © 2025 by The Overflow Group

All rights reserved. No portion of this book may be reproduced, stored in a retrieval system, or transmitted in any form or by any means — electronic, mechanical, photocopying, recording, scanning, or otherwise — without prior written permission of the publisher, except for brief quotations used in reviews, articles, or scholarly works.

www.ingramcontent.com/pod-product-compliance
Lightning Source LLC
Chambersburg PA
CBHW050908160426
43194CB00011B/2330